ENCYCLOPAEDIA OF EMINENT THINKERS

VOLUME-IX: **AMBEDKAR**

Encyclopaedia of Eminent Thinkers Series

Vol. I. The Political Thought of **Mahatma Gandhi**
Vol. II. The Political Thought of **Nehru**
Vol. III. The Political Thought of **Rabindra Nath Tagore**
Vol. IV. The Political Thought of **Radhakrishnan**
Vol. V. The Political Thought of **Vinoba**
Vol. VI. The Political Thought of **Aurobindo**
Vol. VII. The Political Thought of **Jayaprakash Narayan**
Vol. VIII. The Political Thought of **Vivekananda**
Vol. IX. The Political Thought of **Ambedkar**
Vol. X. The Political Thought of **M.N. Roy**

About the Author

K.S. Bharathi did his Master's Degree in Gandhian Thought, Peace-Science, Economics, and Political Science. He also did Postgraduate Diplomas in Politics, Public Administration. Population Dynamics, Gandhian Thought, Tourism, and Telgu. He has contributed some articles in learned journals. He is the author of : *Foundation of Gandhian Thought, Gandhi and Humanity, Socio-Religious Thoughts of Mahatma Gandhi, The Philosophy of Sarvodya, The Satyagràha of Mahatma Gandhi, Gandhi and Nehru, Foundations of Ambedkar Thought, The Social Philosophy of Mahatma Gandhi, Gandhian Approach to Rural Development, The Relevance of Gandhi, Gandhi and Vinoba, The Philosophical Foundations of Gandhian Thought, The Political Thought of Gandhi, The Economic Thought of Gandhi, The Social Thought of Gandhi,* and *The Quintessence and Chronology of Gandhi*. At present, he is the Head of the Postgraduate Department of Gandhian Thought of Nagpur University. He is the Chairman of the Board of Studies of Gandhian Thought, member of the Academic Council, member of the Faculty of Social Sciences, member of the Board of Examination, and member of the Doctoral Research Committee of Nagpur University.

ENCYCLOPAEDIA OF EMINENT THINKERS

VOLUME-NINE

THE POLITICAL THOUGHT OF AMBEDKAR

K. S. BHARATHI
Head, P.G. Department of Gandhian Thought,
Nagpur University, Nagpur

CONCEPT PUBLISHING COMPANY, NEW DELHI-110059

ISBN 81-7022-684-8 (Series)

ISBN 81-7022-710-0 (Vol. 9)

First Published 1998

Published and Printed by
Ashok Kumar Mittal
Concept Publishing Company
A/15-16, Commercial Block, Mohan Garden,
NEW DELHI - 110059 (India)

Phones : 5648039, 5649024
Fax : 011-5598898

TO
MY NEPHEW

S. J. SIVAPRAKASH

PREFACE

There are many valuable books on Ambedkar. There is hardly any book attempting a comprehensive exposition and evaluation of the Political Thought of Ambedkar. This work seeks to provide a comprehensive exposition of the Political Thought of Ambedkar in a precise and lucid manner.

Ambedkar was a lawyer, a professor, an educationist, a parliamentarian, a social reformer and a leveller. His political ideas are gathered from his basic writings. He disliked inane political ideals and he made corrections in his ideas and ideals pragmatically with a critical mind.

In Ambedkar's approach, there is a combination of thought and action, which helped him in formulating his ideas and ideals. His political thought, in a sense, is an expression of important human affairs and is a sincere attempt to bridge the gap between practice and theory, materialism and spiritualism.

Aurobindo regards organised religion as more an obstacle than a help to a fair and honest political life. His political thought recognises nationalism as a fact, though India's nationalism is not an aggressive nationalism. He champions the cause of human freedom, because without freedom, there can be no good and happy life. He regards imperialism of any sort as the enemy of all progress, peace and prosperity. His political thought regards democracy as the best means for realising human values and it condemns fascism and totalitarianism. He has an immense faith in the principle of non-violence. His political thought stresses the need of love and knowledge.

I would like to place on record my indebtedness to scholars and thinkers whose ideas enabled me to bring out this book. I gratefully acknowledge the scholars from whose work I have drawn citations viz., Dr. B.G. Tiwari, Dr. Dhananjay Keer, Dr. Jatava and Dr. Ambedkar.

So far as the writing of this book is concerned, whatever success I have achieved is due to the relentless efforts and encouragement of my friend, philosopher and guide, Dr. P.S.G. Kumar, Head,

Department of Library and Information Science, Nagpur University. I sincerely express my gratitude to him.

I am indebted to Mr. Ashok Kumar Mittal, Concept Publishing Company for publishing this book in such a short span of time. Finally, I hold myself to blame for the errors and shortcomings if any. This work would have not been completed without the grace of Lord Venkateswara of Tirumala and Alamelu Thayar of Tiruchanur.

CONTENTS

1

LIFE AND WORK OF AMBEDKAR

Ambedkar was a multi-dimensional man of genius. He was a brilliant academician, a popular attorney, an erudite scholar, a great legal luminary, a powerful writer, a journalist, a great constitutional pundit, emancipator and champion of the rights and liberties of the dumb, down-trodden and oppressed people. Social justice was his mission of life. He was not so much a reformer as a revolutionary. He will be remembered most of all as a great and compassionate social rebel, a militant reformer and a liberator of the downtrodden masses of the sub-continent, but he was at the same time a democrat and rejected outright the Marxian theory of dictatorship of the proletariat. But he believed that no democratic process could be complete unless masses were properly educated. He was a great educationist. He was a thinker, a critic, a dreamer, a rebel, an emancipator and what not.

Ambedkar hailed from a poor family belonging to one of the Hindu untouchable communities in India. The untouchables had different names in different parts of the country. His ancestral's village is Ambavade, a small town in the Ratnagiri District. His grand-father Maloji Sakpal came from a good Mahar family. Maloji Sakpal was a retired military man. He had fourteen children. Ambedkar was the fourteenth child of his parents. His original name was Bhimrao. He was born on 14 April, 1891. Within two years of Bhim's birth, his father retired from military and the family moved to Satara and then on to Bombay. His mother expired when he was only six years. His father lived a very industrious and intensely religious life.[1]

Ramji Sakpal read and recited to his children the great national epics, the *Ramayana* and the *Mahabharata* the two unfailing sources of divine inspiration, the motive force, which have nurtured and moulded the lives of great men in India in every generation. He also sang the spiritual songs of the Marathi saint poets. He was not merely interested in the spiritual development of his children but also cared for the worldly betterment of his sons. He was a full-fledged teacher. He served as a Headmaster for fourteen years in the military school. He was a confirmed teetotallar and never touched meat. He took keen interest in religious discussions.

Bhimrao was sent to a Marathi school in Dapoli at the age of five. He was admitted to the Government High School, Satara in 1900. Here his name was registered as Bhiva Ramji Ambavadekar. A teacher named Ambedkar in the Satara High School, loved Bhimrao very much. As a mark of love and respect to this teacher, Bhimrao began to call himself Ambedkar. As a boy he was meted out a separatist and inhuman treatment. Bhim and his brother were usually made to squat in a corner of the class on a piece of gunny cloth which they carried to school. The teachers would not touch their notebooks, nor did some of them even ask them to recite poems or put questions to them for fear of being polluted. When these two boys felt thirsty in the school they turned their mouth upward and then somebody would kindly pour drinking water into their mouths as if through a funnel. Bhim had little or no love for his studies.

Bhimrao's father married a second time. Bhim did not like this. He now decided that he must not depend upon his father for maintenance and must earn his own bread. He decided to go to Bombay in order to get job in mills. In order to go to Bombay, with money, he thought out a plan to steal the purse of his aunt. "For three successive nights I tried to remove the purse tucked up at the waist of my aunt, but without success. On the fourth night I did get hold of the purse, but to my disappointment I found only half an anna in it. And in half an anna, of course, I could not go to Bombay. The four nights experience was so nerve-racking that I gave up the idea of collecting money. In this shameful manner and I came to another decision—a decision that gave an entirely different turn to my life."[2]

Ramji Sakpal shifted to Bombay in 1904. He got his sons admitted into the Maratha High School. Bhim had made much progress with his studies. Instead of studying class books he showed keen interest in reading other books. His father supplied him with new books. He was sent to the Elphinstone High School in Bombay. He studied hard now. His father took a personal interest in his studies. The atmosphere in the school was not free from casteism. There were the same prejudices and the same hatreds. The school was a miniature reflection of the vast insulting world outside. The untouchables were prohibited from learning Sanskrit. During his school days both Bhim's elder brother and he were not allowed to take up Sanskrit as a second language. Bhim and his brother were alienated from Sanskrit by the Brahmin teachers. Later on, he studied Sanskrit partly by himself and sometimes with the help of some pandits and himself become a pandit.

Ambedkar passed his matriculation examination in 1907. He obtained 282 out of 750 marks. His success was celebrated by the depressed classes. K. A. Keluskar presented him with his new book *The Life of Gautama Buddha.* He was also instrumental in arranging an interview between him and the Maharaja of Baroda. The Maharaja of Baroda sanctioned him Rs. 25 per month for higher education. Ambedkar was married to Rambai when he was only fourteen. After passing his matriculation examination, he joined the Elphinstone College. Prof. Muller gave him books and clothes. He passed his B.A. examination in 1912. He joined the Baroda State forces as a lieutenant. His father breathed his last on 2 February, 1913. It was a great shock to him. He did not like to go back to Baroda. He had to face a lot of humiliation in the office. He had to resign his post.

Ambedkar was selected as a Gaekwad scholar. He agreed to serve in Baroda State after receiving his education abroad. So, he left India for the United States of America in June 1913. He joined the Columbia University. He studied economics, sociology, history, philosophy, anthropology and political science. His stay in Columbia enlarged his mental vision. He obtained his M.A. degree in 1915 for his thesis, *Ancient Indian Commerce.* He worked on a thesis for Ph.D in economics. In 1916, he submitted his thesis for Ph.D. entitled, *National Dividend for India: A Historic and Analytical Study.* He was awarded the degree of Doctor of Philosophy for his work on 8 June 1917. He left Columbia University in June 1916 and joined the London School of Economics and Political Science. Prof. Seligman helped him. He had to leave the studies in the middle as the scholarship was terminated and he was called back to India by the Dewan of Baroda.

Ambedkar returned to Bombay on 21 August, 1917. He was appointed Secretary to the Maharaja of Baroda. He was not treated well by the staff of the Baroda State. His birth as an untouchable turned everything topsy-turvy. He was treated by his staff and peons as a leper. Peons refused to serve even drinking water to him in the office. This demoralising atmosphere frustrated him. He started to find out a suitable job in Bombay. He was unemployed for about a year. He was using his time for intellectual pursuits. He gave tuitions to two students. He worked under a Parsi businessman.

In November 1918, Ambedkar joined Sydenham College as a Professor of Political Economics and worked there for 2 years. His profundity of knowledge, and convincing style of leactures earned him popularity amongst students. But the social treatment remained unchanged. Some Gujarati professors objected to his drinking water from the pot reserved for the professional staff. He had resigned from his post. He had saved some money and proceeded to England. He joined the London School of Economics and Political Science and also kept terms for the Bar at the Gray's Inn. He studied very hard. He turned his attention to the London Museum. In the museum, he poured over books from morning till evening. Time was an important factor to him. To save both money and time, he would go without lunch. During these studies in London for his academic eminence, he had not forgotten the real aim in his life.

Ambedkar submitted his thesis on Provincial Decentralisation of Imperial Finance in British India. He was awarded the Master of Science in June, 1921, for his thesis. In October 1922, he submitted another thesis, the Problem of the Rupee, to the University of London. He went to the Bonn University, Germany for studies. The thesis was returned and he was asked to rewrite the thesis without changing the conclusions, which he did. He obtained the D.Sc degree. In December 1923, the thesis was published. In April 1923, he was called to the bar.

Ambedkar started legal practice in Bombay from June 1923, and joined the Appellate side of the Bombay Bar. Here also he had to suffer humiliation due to the stigma of his caste. He got very few cases but he continued his efforts. He was helped by N.M. Joshi and D. A. Khare. He worked in Batliboi's Accountancy Institute as a professor of Mercantile Law on a part-time basis for three years. He demanded separate electorates and reserved seats in proportion to the untouchables population. He wanted to organise the untouchables under one banner. So, he established an organisation, the Bahishkrit Hitkarini Sabha on 20 July, 1924. He presided at the Provincial Depressed Classes Conference held at Nipani on 10 and 11 April, 1925. It was at this place that he publicly asserted that Gandhiji was not giving to the untouchability problem the stress that he was giving to *Khadi* propagation and Hindu-Muslim unity. On 4 January, 1925, a hostel was inaugurated for the untouchable school boys.

Ambedkar started a paper entitled "Bahishkrit Bharat" which voiced the grievances of the depressed classes. He launched a successful *satyagraha* at Mahad in the Kolaba district where untouchables were denied access to a tank. He gave evidence in 1926 before the Royal Commission on Currency and Finance and was nominated along with Dr. Solanki on the Bombay Legislative Council in 1927. He was also invited to Ahilya Ashram, Poona, where a big students conference was held. It was in this meeting that the 'Samta Sangh Party' of the students was established, with the aim of improving discipline and self-control amongst the students. He stressed the need for organising the Hindu society on the principle of human rights and equality for all. Resolutions were passed in the conference. The conference declared the *Manusmriti,* a gospel of physical, and mental serfdom of the *Shudras*. The resolution moved by him about *satyagraha* was passed.

Ambedkar introduced a Bill in the Bombay Legislative Council for the amendment of the Hereditary Offices Act, 1874 on 19 March, 1928. This act required that Mahars should work day and night in the service of the Hindus. In exchange they got a very small piece of land called *Uatan Land*, some coins from the villagers and a 'paltry pittiance' varying from two *annas* to a rupee and half per mensem. In order to break the shackles of serfdom, he introduced the Bill. He explained the Mahar's position to the Government. The Muslim members opposed the Bill and so he had to withdraw the Bill. On 29 May, 1928, he submitted to Simon Commission, a statement concerning the safeguards for the protection of the Depressed classes as a minority in the Bombay presidency. Regarding the representation for the depressed classes, he stated that the Bahishkrit Hitkarnini Sabha was opposed to the principle of nomination.

Ambedkar demanded protection through guarantee as follows:

"(1) That the education of the depressed classes shall be recognised as the first change on the revenue of the province and that an equitable and just proportion of the total grant for education should be earmarked for the benefit of the depressed classes.

(2) That the right of the depressed classes to unrestricted recruitment in the army, navy and the police shall be recognised without any limitations as to cost.

(3) That for a period of 30 years the right of the depressed classes for priority in the matter of recruitments to all posts, gazetted as well as non-gazetted, in all civil services shall be recognised

(4) That the right of the depressed classes to the appointment of a special inspector of police from amongst themselves for every District shall be recognised.

(5) That the right of the depressed classes to effective representation on the local Bodies shall be recognised by the Provincial Governments.

(6) That the right of the depressed classes to appeal to the Government of India, in case of violation of these rights by the Provincial Governments shall be recognised and the Government of India shall be given the powers to compel the Provincial Governments to confirm to the law in the matter."[3]

An All-India Depressed Classes Congress was held at Nagpur on 8 August, 1930. Ambedkar presided over the Congress. He said, "A Common Government is often the best instrument one can devise to mould a diverse people into a nation . . . Historically, as well as logically it seems to me not open to any one to urge that the diversity of conditions and people puts a bar in the way of India's self-government. Indeed, if the ideal is that India should be a united nation, I venture to say, self-government would be the most potent instrument for the realisation of that ideal".[4]

Ambedkar emphasised the necessity of the depressed classes entry in public services of the country. He complained that the Simon Commission had systematically under-evaluated the needs and the claims of depressed classes. His participation in the Round Table Conference played an important role in bringing him into the limelight as the leader of the untouchables of India. He pointed out the shortcomings of the British attitude towards the depressed classes. He demanded rights of equal citizenship with the other citizens of India, abolition of untouchability and all other forms of discrimination and legal disability. He supported the demand of Dominion status along with other nationalities.

Ambedkar was Gandhi's most ruthless critic. His charge against Gandhi and the Congress was that they did not care for the untouchables. They did not show a change of heart so far as the untouchables and the depressed classes were concerned. He wanted separate electorate for the untouchables but Gandhi opposed it. He demanded legislation against social persecution. He demanded the right to adequate representation in legislature by election and not by nomination. He negotiated with the other minority representatives and signed a pact, known as the Minorities Pact, after mutual agreement.

Ambedkar returned to Bombay on 28 December, 1931. His work at the Second Round Table Conference was fully satisfied by the Depressed classes in India. Meanwhile in India, the Minority Pact was disliked by Mr. Rajah. He published a statement informing the public about the origin of Rajah-Moonje Pact. He wrote a letter to M.G.A. Gavai. He wrote, "I was shocked to find out that Mr. Rajah has changed his opinion and is now advocating joint electorates. I hope your Association will not follow him in this policy which is suicidal in every way but if it does then you must take the consequences of a permanent breach between us and a war among ourselves which I am trying to avoid at any cost. So don't persist in it".[5] He decided to hold an All-India Depressed Classes Congress very soon to record the real opinion of the depressed classes on this issue. The patriotism of Ambedkar was doubted by certain sections of the people. Poona Pact was signed on 24 September, 1932.

According to the Poona Pact, the depressed classes were to forgo their separate electorates and have general Hindu electorates, subject to important safeguards. The Poona Pact settled the very important controversy about leadership. The negotiations during the pact brought out certain standing qualities of Ambedkar. He wrote a letter to Gandhi that he wanted to meet him particularly about the panel system of Poona Pact. Gandhi finally published his views on the benefits of the Panel system in the Poona Pact in *Harijan*. He said, "So far as I can see and so long as the system of reservation prevails, the panel system is the best adopted for securing the selection only of those candidates who in the *Harijan* opinion are best fitted to serve this special interest, whereas I can see nothing but seeds of strife and bitterness in the alternative proposal."[6]

The tussle between Ambedkar and Gandhi rose from a fundamental difference in their approaches to the problem of untouchability and the steps for its eradication. There may be different views about the conflicting approaches adopted by Ambedkar and Gandhi, to solve the problem of untouchability but none can deny their prime contributions in removing the taboos and restraints to the depressed classes. Ambedkar and Gandhi dedicated their lives to the restoration of equality to the *avarna* section of Hindu society.

Ambedkar returned to India on 8 January, 1934. He resumed his legal profession. He also accepted the part-time professor job in the Government Law College, Bombay. His wife expired on 27 May, 1935. He was appointed the post of the principal of the Government Law College, Bombay from 1 June, 1935. He founded a new political party by the name of Independent Labour Party in August, 1936. He opposed the Industrial Disputes Bill in Bombay Legislative Assembly in 1938. Regarding Hindu-Muslim Problem he said that he did not believe in the allegation that the Muslims were being tyrannlyzed or terrorised in the Congress provinces. He stated that he found it very difficult to dissuade his community from merging itself in some other large community.

The depressed classes observed 19 March, 1939 as their Independence Day. Ambedkar said, "I do not agree with Mr. Gandhi and the Congress when they say that India is a nation. I do not agree either with the foreign Relations Committee of the Muslim League when they say that Hindus and Muslims could not be welded together into a nation."[7] He was appointed to the Executive Council of the Governor-General of India in July, 1942 as Labour Member. He held the post till July 1946. On 26 September, 1944, he made the depressed classes stand on the political evaluation of India clearer. He demanded an equal place with Hindus and Muslims in the future constitution.

According to Ambedkar, the executive should cease to be a committee of the majority party in the legislature. The executive should be parliamentary in the sense that the members of executive should be chosen from the members of the legislatures and should have the right to sit in the house, speak, vote and answer questions. The Prime Minister as the Executive Head of the Government should have the confidence of the whole House.

Ambedkar submitted a memorandum before the Cabinet Mission on behalf of the Scheduled Castes Federation. On 29 June, 1946, a caretaker Government was announced. The depressed classes started their agitation asking for a clarification of their rights and representation in a free India. Satyagraha campaigns were launched at Poona, Kanpur and Lucknow simultaneously. He went to London in September 1946, to plead for Constitutional safeguards for the untouchables after withdrawal of the British from India. He was elected to the Constituent Assembly from Bengal in November 1946. In his first speech in the Constituent Assembly, he called for a United India. He urged patience, forbearence and sacrifice of the personal, party and group interests for peace and unity in the country. On 16 July, 1947, he once again opened the controversial topic of joint *versus* separate electorates.

Jawaharlal Nehru included Ambedkar as Law Minister in the new Cabinet. Ambedkar accepted the invitation because he thought he could serve the interests of the Scheduled Castes better from within government, than from without and also because the offer was without any condition. On 29 August, 1947, the Constituent Assembly appointed a Drafting Committee with Ambedkar as the Chairman. He realised that if regional languages were made the state language, then the development of provincial cultures might lead to disunity of India, there being no common bond of language. The Draft Constitution was introduced by him on 4 November, 1948 in the Constituent Assembly. The Constitution was adopted by the Assembly on 26 November, 1949.

To quote Dr. Rajendra Prasad, "Sitting in the chair and watching the proceedings from day to day, I have realised as nobody else could have, with what zeal and devotion the members of the Drafting Committee and specially its chairman Dr. Ambedkar, in spite of his indifferent health, have worked. We could never make a decision which was or could be ever so right as when we put him on the Drafting Committee and made him its Chairman. He has not only justified selection but has added lustre to the work which he has done".[8] Ambedkar submitted the Hindu Code Bill to the Parliament in October 1948. He compared the Hindu Code Bill to milk which has been spoiled by mixture with a bitter acid. On 5 February, 1951 he introduced the Hindu Code Bill. It brought forth various reactions, and many objections. On 20 September, 1951, he vigorously defended the Bill in the Parliament.

Ambedkar resigned from his seat in the cabinet on 25 September, 1951. After his resignation, he started concentrating on the General

Elections due to be held in 1952. He was busy campaigning and canvassing for the Scheduled Castes Federation. He charged the Congress government with corruption. He returned to Bombay on 18 November, 1951. He started campaigning in Bombay. The General Elections were held in January, 1952. He contested from a Bombay constituency. He was defeated by a Congress nominee. He was elected from one of the seventeen seats allotted to the Bombay state in the council of states.

Ambedkar addressed the World Buddhist Conference in Kathmandu in 1949 on Marxism *vs* Buddhism. He founded the Bharatiya Buddha Janasangha in July, 1951 and compiled a Buddhist prayer book *Buddha Upasana Patha.* He was a delegate to the World Buddhist Conference, Rangoon, in 1954. He founded the Bharatiya Buddha Mahasabha in 1955. He was continuously suffering from ill-health. He used to have pain in the legs, insomnia and diabetes. Having long lived alone he now decided to get married again. He married Dr. Miss Sharda Kabir at New Delhi on 15 April, 1948. He attended the Buddhist Conference at Columbo. He spoke to the delegates on the "Rise and Fall of Buddhism in India". Now he decided to embrace Buddhism. On 14 October, 1956, he embraced Buddhism at Nagpur. He was invited to attend the World Buddhist Conference at Kathmandu in Nepal. He attended the Conference. He spoke on Buddha and Karl Marx. He returned to India on 30 November, 1956. On 5 December, 1956, he was with his private Secretary till 11.15 p.m. Next morning it was found out by Mrs. Ambedkar at 6.30 a.m. that her husband had expired. He passed away in sleep.

REFERENCES

1. *Leader,* Allahabad, 14-3-1929.
2. *The Bombay Sentinel,* 20-11-1942.
3. *Memorandum,* Ambedkar Papers, Available in Bombay University Library, Bombay.
4. B. R. Ambedkar, Presidential Address, Nagpur, 8-8-1930.
5. *Leader,* Allahabad, 28-2-1932.
6. *Letter from Ambedkar to Gandhi,* Sabarmati Series, Set No. 7. Letter No. 155.
7. *Times of India,* 6-8-1940.
8. Dhananjay Keer, *Dr. Ambedkar: His Life and Mission,* Popular Prakashan, Bombay, 1962, p. 413.

2

INFLUENCES ON AMBEDKAR

Ambedkar was aware of the ruthless exploitation of the poor going on all over the world. The theory of class struggle was critically appreciated by him. He was influenced by Marx. While pointing out the differences between class and caste, he observed that the downtrodden people in India were the last to be hired and the first to be fired. he was of the opinion that only those who were under the fetters of slavery could themselves removes their slavery. He thought that the key industries should be nationalised. The insurance business, the land and the key industries must be nationalised but the progress must be gradual, that means, through parliamentary methods. He differed from Marx on one point; that the suffering is not only due to economic exploitation but also due to social exploitation.

John Dewey's philosophy of instrumentalism led Ambedkar towards a critical analysis of the concrete problems facing humanity. His pragmatic approach convinced him that any philosophy which sought to offer a way out from the troubles in which humanity was caught must be dynamic and pragmatic. Ambedkar criticised the ancient philosophers of India. He was influenced by Dewey's method of inquiry. He was also influenced by Dewey's activist epistemology. He fully endorsed Dewey's emphasis on education as a means to change the world. He established the people's Education Society in Bombay in 1946 for the depressed classes. Dewey's ideas provided the basis for a systematic analysis of problems relating to politics, economics, society, religion and history.

Ranade gave precedence to social, economic and religious reforms over political reform. He said, "You cannot have a good social system when you find yourselves low in the scale of political rights nor can you be fit to exercise political rights and privileges unless your social system is based on reason and justice. You cannot have a good economic system if your social arrangements are imperfect. If your religious ideals are low and grovelling, you cannot succeed in social, economic or political spheres."

This inter-dependence is not an accident but is the law of our nature."[1] Ambedkar was influenced by Ranade. He agreed with the views of Ranade. The political philosophy of Ranade had an impact on his mind. It made his pragmatic approach to problems systematic and evolutionary.

The political philosophy of Ranade was summed up in three prepositions. Ambedkar said,

"(1) We must not set up as our ideal something which is purely imaginary. An ideal must be such that it must carry the assurance that it is a practicable one,

(2) In politics, sentiments and temperament of the people are more important than intellect and theory. This is particularly so in the matter of framing a Constitution. A Constitution is as much a matter of taste as clothes are. Both must fit, both must please.

(3) In political negotiations the rule must be what is possible. That does not mean that we should be content with what is offered. No, it means that you must not refuse what is offered when you know that your sanctions are inadequate to compel your opponent to concede more."[2]

Ambedkar agreed with the terms of the Poona Pact. By accepting it, he could save the life of Gandhi. He received many threatening letters from the caste Hindus. He said, "As to myself, it is no exaggeration to say that no man was placed in a greater and graver dilemma than I was then. It was a baffling situation. I had to make a choice between two different alternatives. There was before me the duty which I owed as a part of common humanity, to save Gandhi from sure death. There was before me the problem of saving for the untouchables the political rights which the Prime Minister had given them. I responded to the call of humanity and saved the life of Mr. Gandhi by agreeing to alter the Communal Award in a manner satisfactory to Mr. Gandhi. This agreement is known as the Poona Pact".[3]

According to Ambedkar, Ranade was not only wise but also logical. He said, "you cannot be liberal by halves. You cannot be liberal in politics and conservative in religion. The heart and the head must go together. You cannot cultivate your intellect, enrich your mind, enlarge the sphere of your political rights and privileges and at the same time keep your hearts closed and cramped. It is an ideal dream to expect man to remain unshackled in their own superstition and social evils, while they are struggling hard to win rights and privileges from their rulers. Before long these vain dreamers will find their dreams lost".[4] He also stressed that social reform in order to be lasting must precede political reforms.

Ambedkar was very much influenced by Gandhi. He made efforts to cooperate with him in the removal of untouchability programme in 1924. He got the *Satyagraha* technique from him. He opposed Gandhism. He said, "Gandhism may be well suited to society which does not accept democracy as its ideal. A society which does not believe in democracy may be indifferent to machinery and civilisation based upon it but a democratic society cannot. The former may well content itself with a life of leisure and culture for the few and life to toil and drudgery for many. But a democratic society must assure a life of leisure and culture to each one of its citizens".[5]

According to Ambedkar, "Gandhism insists upon class structure. It regards the class structure of society and also the income structure as sacrosanct with the consequent distinctions of rich and poor, high and low, owners and workers as permanent parts of social organisation. From the point of view of social consequences nothing can be more pernicious. Psychologically, class structure sets in motion . . . There is no common plane on which the privileged and the subject classes can meet. There is no endosmosis, no give and take of life's hopes and experiences. The social and moral evils of this separation to the subject class are of course real and obvious. It educates them into slaves and creates all the psychological complex which follows from a slave mentality. The isolation and exclusiveness following upon the class structure creates in the privileged classes the anti-social spirit of a gang".[6]

Ambedkar was prepared to accept the majority rule in India. He preferred the introduction of adult franchise among a predominantly illiterate people. To quote M.V. Pylee, "while everybody recognises the necessity of diffusion of constitutional morality for the peaceful working of a democratic Constitution, there are two things inter-connected with it which are not unfortunately, generally recognised. One is that the form of administration has a close connection with the form of the Constitution. The form of the administration must be appropriate to and in the same sense as the form of the Constitution. The other is that it is perfectly possible to pervert the Constitution, without changing its form by merely changing the form of the administration and to make it inconsistent and opposed to the spirit of the Constitution. . . Constitutional morality is not a natural sentiment. It has to be cultivated".[7]

Ambedkar pleaded in the Constituent Assembly for compromise between the opposite groups. He said, "If anybody has it in his mind that this problem can be solved by way, or the Muslims may be subjugated, made to surrender to the Constitution that might be prepared without their knowledge and consent this country would be involved in perpetually conquering them. Let us prove by our conduct that we have not only power but also wisdom to carry all sections of the country to march on that road which is bound to lead us to unity".[8]

Ambedkar was not a devotee either of Gandhi or Jinnah. Regarding his opinion about Gandhi and Jinnah, he said, "I am condemned because I criticised Mr. Gandhi and Mr. Jinnah for the mess they have made of Indian politics, and that in doing so I am alleged to have shown towards them hatred and disrespect. In reply to this charge what I have to say is that I have been a critic and I must continue to be such. It may be I am making mistakes but I have always felt that it is better to make mistakes than to accept guidance and direction from others or to sit silent and allow things to deteriorate. Those who have accused me of having been actuated by feelings of hatred forget two things. In the first place this alleged hatred is not born of anything that can be called personal. If I am against them it is because I want a settlement of some sort and I am not prepared to wait for an ideal settlement. Nor can I tolerate anyone on whose will and consent settlement depends to stand on dignity and play the Grand Moghul. In the second place, no one can hope to make any effective mark upon his time and bring the aid that is worth bringing to great principles and struggling causes if he is not strong in his love and his hatred. I hate injustice, tyranny, pompousness, and humbug and my hatred embraces all those who are guilty of them. For these reasons I tender no apology for my criticism of Mr. Gandhi and Mr. Jinnah, the two men who have brought India's political progress to a stand still."[9]

Ambedkar was also influenced by Buddha. Buddha's doctrines of *Annicca* and *Annatta* exercised a profound influence on him. The impact of the teachings of Buddha can be seen in his speeches and writings. To him untouchability was not a bye-product of blood or race inferiority. He ceaselessly strove to raise the mental stature of the downtrodden masses by encouraging them to have faith and hope in their creative potentialities. He laid great emphasis on the individual as the centre of all doctrines and activities. He appreciated Buddha's belief in man's capacity to work out his salvation without extraneous aid. He did not accept the view that impersonal forces are everything and that man is no factor in the making of history. He tested the veracity of the *Vedas*, the Brahmans and the social organisation based on *Chaturvarna.* He interpreted these doctrines in his Buddha and his Dhamma.

Ambedkar remarked that Buddha revolted against the *Vedas* and the Brahmanas because they assumed that: (1) the *Vedas* are not only sacred but that they are infallible and are not to be questioned, (2) that salvation of the soul, or escape from transmigration, can be had only by the due performance of Vedic sacrifices, religious ceremonies and the offering of gifts to Brahmins, (3) that the ideal religion is contained in the *Vedas* alongwith a theory for an ideal society, and (4) that the pattern of this ideal society is based on *Chaturvarna.*

The *Chaturvarna* society advocated the following rules:

(1) Society should be divided into four classes-Brahmins, Kshatriyas, Vaishyas and Shudras.
(2) There cannot be social equality among these four classes. They must be bound together by the rule of graded inequality.
(3) The four classes should observe a division of occupations. The occupations of the Brahmin should be learning and teaching and the performance of religious ceremonies. The occupations of the Kshatriyas, Vaishyas and Shudras should be fighting, trade and service to the three superior classes respectively. These occupations assigned to different classes should be exclusive to each.
(4) The right to education is given to the Brahmins, Kshatriyas and Vaishyas. The Shudras and the women have no right to education.
(5) A man's life is divided into four stages, *Brahmacharya, Grahast, Vanaprastha* and *Sanyasa.*"[10]

Buddha followed the doctrine of egalitarianism and humanism. His indomitable faith in the capacity of man to shape his own destiny appears to have been the most decisive factor which exercised a lasting influence on Ambedkar. His idea that birth is the cause of death might have led him away from the obscurantist trappings of religious mysticism.

One of the important planks of J. R. Phooley's social reform was the education of women and Shudras. He believed that with the dissemination of knowledge light would come to them. He believed that it was their ignorance due to which their low condition had continued. So, he opened schools for girls. Ambedkar wanted to provide opportunities to the suppressed classes to raise themselves socially, economically and politically. He held J. R. Phooley in great admiration due to his work. He believed that the *Manusmriti* had bound the Shudras hand and foot and unless they revolted against it, they would never be able to shake off the shackles of bondage. He dedicated his book *Who Were the Shudras?* to the memory of J. R. Phooley.

Ambedkar was also influenced by *Mill Like Mill,* he was also convinced that unless men are free to form and maintain their own opinions, they cannot develop that mental well-being on which everybody depends. Freedom of thought is absolutely indispensable although freedom of action may be limited. That the actions of an individual must not become a nuisance was pointed out by him in his forceful statement before the Constituent Assembly while dealing with the exceptions and qualifications of the Fundamental Rights. He said, "In the opinion of the critics fundamental rights are not fundamental unless they are also absolute rights. The critics rely on the constitution of the United States and the Bill of Rights embodied in the first ten Amendments to that Constitution in support of their contention. It is said that the fundamental rights in the American Bill of Rights are real because they are not subject to limitations".[11]

Personal humiliation and inhuman treatment made Ambedkar search for ways to reconstruct society on the lines of social democracy. Dhananjay Keer said, "what an indelible impression these cruel disabilities must have made upon Bhim's young mind that was so strong, so sensitive and yet so resolute. Under the pressure of all sorts of such disabilities and maltreatment attendent on the birth of an untouchable of humble rank, Bhim was cultivating a spirit of patience in the school of experience. It is said that letters cut into the bark of a young tree grow with age. All such insulting refusals and ill-treatment must have engendered in him a burning hatred for Hinduism. It was thus in his boyhood that Bhim experienced at the hands of his co-religionists the galling humiliations and the inhuman treatment under which his whole community had been labouring for untold ages."[12]

Ambedkar's interest in religion, his approach and attitude towards social problems, his readings habit, etc., can be traced back to his father. Under his inspiration he came up in his life. The formative period of Ambedkar's life was full of impacts and influences. These influences were many and varied, ranging from personal sufferings to the impact of social reformers.

REFERENCES

1. T.V. Parvade, *Mahadev Govind Ranade,* Asia Publishing House, Bombay, 1963, pp. 276-77.
2. B. R. Ambedkar, *Ranade, Gandhi and Jinnah,* Bheem Patrika Publications, Jullunder, pp. 39-40.
3. B. R. Ambedkar, *What Congress and Gandhi Have done to the Untouchables,* Thacker & Co. Ltd., Bombay, 1945, p. 88.
4. B. R. Ambedkar, Ranade, Gandhi and Jinnah, *op.cit.,* pp. 28-29.
5. B. R. Ambedkar, *What Congress and Gandhi Have done to the Untouchables, op. cit.,* p. 284.
6. *Ibid.,* p. 285.

7. M.V. Pylee, *Constitutional Government in India,* Asia Publishing House, Bombay, 1965, pp. 7-8.
8. Dhananjay Keer, *Dr. Ambedkar: His Life and Mission,* Popular Prakashan, Bombay, 1962, p. 387.
9. B. R. Ambedkar, *Preface to Ranade, Gandhi and Jinnah, op. cit.*
10. B. R. Ambedkar, *The Buddha and His Dhamma,* Siddharth College Publication, Bombay, 1957, pp. 88-89.
11. M. V. Pylee, *Constitutional Government in India, op. cit.,* p. 18.
12. Dhananjay Keer, *Dr. Ambedkar: His Life and Mission, op. cit.,* p. 13.

3

AMBEDKAR ON NATION AND NATIONALISM

The real basis of nationalism is cultural, something spiritual. Nationalism is man made, and therefore, it is closely related with man's life, pride and activity. Nationalism is a force in the history of mankind. To Ambedkar, in whatever way the matter is viewed and howsoever, ardently, one may wish for the elimination of nationalism, nationalism is a fact in human society. He said, "Nationalism is a fact which can neither be eluded nor denied. Whether one calls it an irrational instinct or positive hallucination, the fact remains that it is a potent force which has a dynamic power to disrupt empires. Whether nationalism is the cause or the threat to nationalism is the cause, is a difference of emphasis only."[1] He regards nationalism as a real force in human life.

According to Ambedkar, nationalism has taught much to humanity. He said, "The turks were bound to the Arabs with the ties of religion. The religious tie of Islam is the strongest known to humanity. No social confederacy can claim to rival the Islamic brotherhood at the point of solidarity. But Arab nationalism broke the bonds of Islam and fought against his fellow Muslim, the Turk, for its independence. It won, but Turkey was completely dismantled".[2] In fact, nationalism sometimes is so blind that it causes enmity and anger even among those who have lived together for countries past. Muslim nationalism was so irrationally intense that it disrupted the long and aged unity of Indian people.

Ambedkar recognises the efficacy of nationalism as one of the most dynamic forces of the modern history. National unity was the fundamental aim of his political thought. The spirit of his nationalism started with the humanistic cause of the poorest of poor in the world. He wanted equality and civil rights for those who were deprived of them for centuries past. He emerged as the champion of the downtrodden people. His nationalism was not merely an empty state of mind, but it was based on a full-blooded humanistic faith in the greatness of his country and the dignity of its denizens. He held the British rule responsible for the negligence of the welfare of millions of people.

According to Ambedkar, internal oppression was a gradation of castes forming an ascending scale of reverence and descending scale of contempt. It was a system which gave no scope for the growth of that sentiment of equality and fraternity so essential for a democratic form of government. He emphasised the point that the political mechanism must take account of these poor classes of untouchables. He wanted some constitutional safeguards to protect the unprotected, to give heart to the heartless, to provide relief to the weary and succour to the suppressed, and nothing more. His attitude was humanistic as well as nationalist. He wanted not only freedom from foreign domination, but also internal freedom for the people whom it was denied. He said, "We must have a Government in which men in power knowing where obedience will end and resistance will begin, will not be afraid to amend the social and economic code of life which the dictates of justice and expediency so urgently call for. This Role of the British Government will never be able to play. It is only a government which is of the people, for the people and by the people that will make this possible".[3]

Nationalism does not mean communalism to Ambedkar. It means the spirit of oneness in the people. He was opposed to the wrong social structure of India's past, but to say he was against the nation is wholly wrong. He said, "I know my position has not been understood properly in the country. It has often been misunderstood . . . I say that whenever there has been a conflict between my personal interests and the interests of the country as a whole, I have always placed the claim of the country above my personal claims. I have never pursued the path of private gain . . . so far as the demands of the country are concerned, I have never lagged behind".[4] His spirit of nationalism took a definite shape through the struggle against the British rule. The struggle against foreign domination and love for the community in which he was born, brought in his mind the real implications of nationalism.

Ambedkar likes to use the word nation in that sense which points out to the area of society rather than that of the State. He said, "Philosophically, it may be possible to consider a nation as a unit but sociologically it cannot but be regarded as consisting of many classes and the freedom of the nation, if it is to be a reality, must vouchsafe the freedom of the different classes comprised in it, particularly of those who are treated as the servile classes."[5] In his view, a nation consists of at least two things. First, a nation includes the whole society, in all the varied range of life, these different social classes also have an attachment to the tradition and achievement. Secondly, a country comprises of an area of soil, which is the physical feature of the land these social classes occupy. Thus the nation is made of two factors—society and the land it resides on.

Ambedkar makes a clear distinction between the freedom of the country and of the people of that country, which the western writers on political science overlook. To him, the freedom of a country is one thing and the freedom of the people living in that country is another. He emphasised on the freedom of both. Freedom of a country, without the freedom of its people, is not true freedom. His main stress was on the freedom of the people. Without the freedom of people, nationalism becomes a means of internal slavery, forced labour and organised tyranny for the poor and servile classes.

According to Ambedkar, the unity of the country was not simply theoretical and intellectual. It was practical and secular. He said, "I have not the slightest doubt about the future evolution of the social, political and economic structure of this country. I know today, we are divided politically, socially and economically. We are in warring camps, and I am probably one of the leaders of a Warring Camp. With all this I am convinced that given time and circumstances, nothing in the world will prevent this country from becoming one and with all our castes and creeds, I have not the slightest hesitation in saying that we shall in some form be united people".[6]

Ambedkar had an immense faith in the bright future and evolution of his country. Even during the talks of achieving freedom for India, his ultimate goal was how to unite the people. He said, "So far as the ultimate goal is concerned, none of us have any apprehension or doubt. Our difficulty was not about the ultimate thing but how to unite the heterogeneous mass that we are today to take a decision in common and march in a cooperative way on that road, which is bound to lead us to unity".[7] He discouraged all heterogeneity, doubts and differences and appealed to the people of India for social and national unity. He said, "I should have thought, therefore, that in order to make a start and in order to induce every part and every section in this country to cooperate, it would be an act of the greatest statesmanship for the majority part even to make a concession to the prejudices of the people who are not prepared to march together, and it is for that, I propose to make this appeal. Let us leave aside slogans which frighten people. Let us even make concessions to the prejudices of our opponents. Bring them in, so that they may willingly join this march on that road which must necessarily lead us to unity".[8]

Ambedkar wants the spiritual unity of the people. He said, "What is wanted is not merely political unity but a true union of heart and soul, in other words, social unity. Political unity is worth nothing, if it is not the expression of real union. It is as precarious as the unity between persons, who without being friends become allies of each other . . . personally, I do not think that a permanent union can be made to depend upon the satisfaction of mere material interests".[9] It is clear that the unity of the country, not only political and social, but also spiritual, was the supreme concern of his freedom movement.

National feeling is a feeling of consciousness of kind. It is in a sense belonging together and leaving aside the rest. Ambedkar said, "It is a feeling of a corporate sentiment of oneness which makes those who are charged with it feel that they are kith and kin. This national feeling is a double-edged feeling. It is at once a feeling of fellowship for one's own kith and kin and an anti-fellowship feeling for those who are not one's own kith and kin."[10] It is essentially a double-edged feeling. He said, "A feeling of consciousness of kind which is on the one hand binds together those who have it, so strongly that it overrides all differences arising out of economic conflicts or social gradations and, on the other hand, severs them from those who are not of their kind. It is a feeling not to belong to any other group. This is the essence of what is called a nationality and national feeling".[11]

Nationalism is an obstacle to international understanding and fellowship. Though to Ambedkar, national feeling is both a fellowship and an anti-fellowship element, there is no room for race-hatred, caste-feeling, and social prejudices in his concept of nationalism. He would definitely agree with Swami Vivekananda who preached, "I am thoroughly convinced that no individual or nation can live by holding itself apart from the community of others, and wherever such an attempt has been made under false ideas of greatness, policy or holiness—the result has always been disastrous to the secluding one. The fact of our isolation from all the other nations of the world is the cause of our degeneration and its only remedy is getting back into the current of the rest of the world. Motion is the sign of life".[12] To Ambedkar, national feeling is not merely negative. It is essentially positive, if the people long to live together.

There is a difference between nationality and nationalism. They are two different psychological states of human mind. Ambedkar says that nationality means consciousness of kind, awareness of the existence of that kinship. He said, "The feeling of nationality may be present and yet the feeling of nationalism may be quite absent. That is to say, nationality does not, in all cases, produce nationalism".[13] To him, nationality can flare up into nationalism only when two conditions are present:

(1) There must arise the will to live as a nation. Nationalism is a dynamic expression of that desire.

(2) There must be a territory which nationalism could occupy and make it a State, as well as a cultural home of the nation. Without such a territory, nationalism would be a soul, as it were, wandering in search of a body in which to begin life over again and dies out finding none.

According to Ambedkar, "Nationalism is not a matter of political nexus or cash nexus, for the simpel reason that union cannot be the result of calculation of mere externals. Where two communities live a life which is exclusive and self-enclosed for five years, they will not be one, because, they are made to come together on one day in five years for the purposes of voting in an election".[14] What he wants is social unity among the varied modes of human life. Social unity is essential to bind the people together because with mere political unity, India may be a state. He said, "But to be a state is not to be a nation and a state, which is not a nation, has small prospects of survival in the struggle for existence. This is especially true where nationalism—the most dynamic force of modern times—is seeking everywhere to free itself by the destruction and disruption of all mixed states".[15] True nationalism must satisfy social unity and human brotherhood.

Ambedkar makes a clear distinction between a nation and a community. To him, a right to insurrection is restricted only to insisting on a change in the mode and manner of government; the right of disruption is greater than the right of insurrection and extend to the secession of a group of the members of a state with a secession of the portion of the state's territory in its occupation. The political thinkers have not given reason why the right of one is limited to insurrection and why that of the other extends to disruption. He said, "To my mind, the reason for this difference pertains to questions of ultimate destiny. A state either consists of a series of communities or it consists of a series of nations. In a state, which is composed of a series of communities, one community may be arrayed against another community and the two may be opposed to each other. But in the matter of their ultimate destiny they feel they are one. But in a state, which is composed of a series of nations, when one nation rises against the other, the conflict is one as to differences of ultimate destiny".[16]

Regarding the distinction between a community and a nation, Ambedkar said, "That a community, however, different from and, however, opposed to other communities, major or minor, is one with the rest in the matter of the ultimate destiny of all. A nation, on the other hand, is not only different from other components of the state but it believes in and cherishes a different destiny totally antagonistic to the destiny entertained by other component elements in the state".[17] He defined the two terms, community and nation. He said, "A people who, notwithstanding their differences accept a common destiny for themselves as well as for their opponents, are a community. A people who are not only different from the rest but who refuse to accept for themselves the same destiny which others do are a nation".[18]

Ambedkar discounts all disruptive tendencies, all superficial distinctions based on different religions and languages, though he admits the disadvantages of such diversity. He has a deep faith in India's cultural unity. He said, "Her unity is as ancient as Nature. Within this geographic unit and covering the whole of it there has been a cultural unity from time immemorial. This cultural unity has defied political and racial divisions. At any rate for the last hundred and fifty years all institutions—cultural, political, economic, legal and administrative—have been working on a single, uniform spring of action. In any discussion . . . the fact cannot be lost sight of, namely, that the starting point, if not the governing factor, is the fundamental unity of India".[19]

Ambedkar recognises the demerits of a diversity of language in a country, but the different languages, to him, should not hinder the growth and spirit of nationalism. One state, one language is a universal feature of almost every state. With a good faith in nationalism, he said, "One language can unite people. Two languages are sure to divide people. This is an inexorable law. Culture is conserved by language. Since Indians wish to unite and develop a common culture it is the bounden duty of all Indians to own up Hindi as their language".[20] In this way, he stresses on the need of a common language. He wants something more from the people of this great country for their own good, unity and welfare. He said, "Any Indian who does not accept this proposal as part and parcel of a linguistic state has no right to be an Indian. He may be a hundred per cent Maharashtrian, a hundred per cent Tamil or a hundred per cent Gujarati, but he cannot be an Indian in the real sense of the word except in a geographical sense.[21] Through one common language, he wishes to have two things—a sense of unity and oneness and a strong feeling of nationalism.

Ambedkar always regards communalism as the most dangerous persistent and pestilential exhibition of a narrow type of faith. It opposes full-blooded nationalism, hampers the happiness of other social groups and mars social unity. In communalism, different communities or religions are involved and so long as one community looks upon the other as menace, there will not be any social progress and political stability. The spirit of conservatism and communalism will continue to dominate the thoughts and actions of all communities. He lays a stress on the need of fighting against separatism, provincialism, linguism, casteism, and communalism.

Casteism, is against the spirit of nationalism. It has weakened India, socially and nationally. Ambedkar said, "caste has killed public spirit. Caste has destroyed the sense of public charity. Caste has made public opinion impossible. Virtue has become caste-ridden and morality has become caste-bound. There is no sympathy to the deserving. There is no appreciation of the meritorious. There is no charity to the needy. Suffering as such calls for no response. There is charity but it begins with the caste and ends with the caste. There is sympathy but not for men of other caste".[22] This caste feeling is the mother of communalism. To him, nationalism means the negation of caste-spirit and caste-sprit is nothing but a deep-rooted communalism.

Communal feelings are a menace to national integration and hamper the way for liberty, equality and fraternity. He is a strong supporter of democratic institutions for the happy future of his nation. His concept of nationalism encourages man to love his country and prepare him to hate all those who are the enemies of country or in any way impede the progress of his nation. To him, nationalism is a spiritual phenomenon rooted in humanism. He is convinced that nationalism is a process of social assimilation and, therefore, nationalism is to receive its perfect harmony in the realisation of social brotherhood of men irrespective of caste, colour and creed.

Ambedkar believes in the Indian nationalism. He does not hold any religious view of nationalism such as Hindu nationalism or Muslim nationalism. He said, "Unfortunately for the minorities in India, Indian nationalism has developed a new doctrine which may be called the Divine Right of the majority to rule the minorities according to the wishes of the majority. Any claim for the sharing of power by the minority is called communalism while the monopolising of the whole power by the majority is called Nationalism".[23] He never allows his nationalistic spirit to submit to such a type of irrationalism.

Ambedkar regards religion as an important part of India's destiny. To him, no religion should disrupt the India's spirit of nationalism and secularism. He accepts the principle of secularism for the future existence of all religions, for all men cannot come under one religious faith. Men cannot live by bread alone; they have a mind which needs proper food for thought; religion instils hope in men and puts them into action. He does not want irrational nationalism in the name of religion. What he wants is that religion should be the binding force which deepens the solidarity of human society. He advocates for religious tolerance and condemns all kinds of hypocrisy and oppression in the name of religion and nationalism.

Patriotism and nationalism are two different though relative terms. To quote E. Barker, "Nationalism, in its proper sense, is a term which belongs to the area of society rather that of the state; it is a feeling of attachment to the tradition and achievement of the whole national society, in all the varid range of its life, just as patriotism (if we distinguish it from nationalism) is a feeling of attachment to the very soil and the physical features of the whole land of our birth or *patria,* in all its sweep and variety."[24] Nationalism and patriotism are such vital ideas that are related to human society. He does not want hypocrisy in the name of nationalism and patriotism. These terms are dynamic and do not induce passivity in the adherents of them. To him, patriotism demands action in right direction and reaction against all wrongs. Mere attachment to the land is half-hearted patriotic spirit.

Ambedkar does not strive for power in the name of patriotism. He said, "I am glad I do not belong to that class of patriots. I belong to that class which takes its stand on democracy and which seeks to destroy monopoly in every shape and form. Our aim is to realise in practice our ideal of one man, one value in all walks of life, political, economic and social."[25] This is the essence of his patriotism. To him, patriotism and nationalism mean democracy, liberty and equality. He stands to total negation of disruptive, sectarian, reactionary, obscurantist and opportunist elements in the national life of Indian society. He advises the people not to support the cruel and corrupt institutions of patriotism and nationalism. Liberty, equality and fraternity prescribe the minimum that all men and women should be entitled to claim in the national society and state.

According to Ambedkar, *Fraternity* stands for love and brotherhood. *Love* is the basis of society around which all the laws and institutions should revolve for ever. His idea of patriotism and nationalism implies economic, political, social and cultural equality and liberty and moral values without which the Indian nation will not flourish and proper. His idea of patriotism and nationalism creates a spirit of social brotherhood and a determination to improve the lot of the people who live in the same country but are not otherwise treated as full men.

Ambedkar is vehemently opposed to the gangster's method in politics. To him, gangsterism means vandalism and vendettas. By it, social and political riots are caused on a large scale. He condemned gangsterism when there was talk of freedom for our country. The spread of gangsterism in the body politic creates a mentality which is sure to bring forth a life and death struggle leading to disunity, disruption and destruction, among the people themselves. Gangsters destroy cohesion, weaken the love and faith of the people and prevent the use, if not retardation of their moral and human resources.

Ambedkar always opposed to the policy of appeasement. He said, "Appeasement means bying off the aggressor by conniving at his acts of murder, rape, arson and loot against innocent persons who happen for the moment to be the victims of his displeasure".[26] What he wants is settlement. Settlement means laying down the bounds which neither party to it can transgress. Appeasement sets no limits to the demands and aspirations of the aggressor. Settlement does. This policy is also known as the policy of concessions. When he talks of settlement, his main emphasis is on the inevitable which must be attended to. He said, "I am one of those who believe that what is inevitable must be faced. There is no use in burying one's head in the sand and refusing to take notice of what is happening round about because the sound of it hurts one's sentiments".[27]

Appeasement, slackness and procrastination in the face of inevitables are such things that cannot give permanent peace to political life. Ambedkar believes in a sincere settlement and appeals to attend to the inevitable, he does not submit at any cost to the wrong. Submission to the wrong, in any sphere of life, spoils the moral stamina of human existence. Settlement is a rational approach to political activities. To him, gangsterism requires submission to the wrong, whereas appeasement is not generally so. Both appeasement and gangsterism prevent the growth and development of honest democratic institutions and humanistic activities. They create a society in which life is not worthwhile.

During the Nineteenth century, the self-determination meant the right to establish a form of government in accordance with the wishes of the people. But at present, self-determination has meant the right to obtain national independence from an alien race irrespective of the form of government. According to Ambedkar, the principle of self-determination has certain limitations. First of these is self-determination must be by the people. The other limitation is the degree of imperative character with which the principle of self-determination can be said to be invested. Another limitation is the issue of self-determination. Self-determination for a nationality may take the form of cultural independence or may take the form of territorial independence.

According to Ambedkar, "If a nationality lives in easily severable and contiguous areas. Other things being equal, a case can be made out for territorial independence. But where owing to inextricable intermingling the nationalities are so mixed up that the areas they occupy are not easily severable, then all that they can be entitled to is cultural independence. Territorial independence in a case like this is an impossibility. They are doomed to live together. The only other alternative they have is to migrate".[28] Such is the definition—the scope and limitations of self-determination in his political thought.

Ambedkar does not wish that he should be worshipped like a hero. He is totally against the hero-worship in the political life of his country, because it prevents a spirit of inquiry, a sense of creativity and an independent attitude of mind. He said, "These ideas of hero-worship will bring ruin on you if you do not nip them in the bud. By defying an individual, you repose faith for your safety and salvation in one single individual with the result that you get into the habit of dependence and indifferent to your duty. If you fall a victim to these ideas, your fate will be no better than logs of wood in the national stream of life. Your struggle will come to naught."[29]

Ambedkar criticises Indian *journalism* for worshipping heroes blindly. He said, "Journalism in India was once a profession. It has now become a trade. It has no more moral function then the manufacture of soap. It does not regard itself as the responsible adviser of the public. To give the news uncloured by any motive, to present a certain view of public policy which it believes to be for the good of the community to correct and chastise without fear all those no matter how high, who have closen a wrong or a barren path, is not regarded by journalism in India as its first or foremost duty."[30]

Ambedkar makes a distinction between admiration and *hero-worship* of man. He said, "Hero-worship in the sense of expressing our unbounded admiration is one thing. To obey the hero is a totally different kind of hero-worship. There is nothing wrong in the former while the latter is no doubt a most pernicious thing".[31] He hopes that his countrymen will some day learn that the country is greater than the men, the heroes, and hero-worship and service to India are two different things. The service to the people is greater than the worship of political heroes.

According to Ambedkar, the defenders and champions of democratic ideals should not lay their liberties at the feet of even a great man or trust him with powers which enables him to subvert their democratic institutions. In fact, hero-worship is against the spirit of democracy. He warns the people against the spirit of irrational and blind hero-worship which prevails in the country.

Nationalism is not a natural desire. It is an acquired habit of love and hate. Ambedkar's spirit of nationalism took shape through his revolt, strivings and struggles against both Indian orthodoxy and British rule, without using any violent method and hostile attitude. To him, nationalism is not the spirit of the whole revivalism of India's past. He stands for getting rid of a crippled and cramped religious outlook, supernatural beliefs and metaphysical speculation. He wants the people to discard what is not good and true in the past and invites them to study the present. His attitude towards nationalism is rational. He does not like extreme nationalism. He knows well that humanity progresses only wnen there is a spirit of cooperation.

According to Ambedkar, under the present circumstances, *nationalism* and *internationalism* have to cooperate in order to mitigate human burden and misery. The spirit of freedom and social emancipation developed in him a strong sense of nationalism. Nationalism appeared as something more than mere political freedom. In building up the Indian nation, he aims at higher things of life. Nationalism is not mere a display of political manoeuvre. The real object of nationalism is the people. Without raising the whole level of the common masses, nationalism cannot long survive.

REFERENCES

1. B.R. Ambedkar, *Pakistan or the Partition of India,* Thacker & Co., Ltd. Bombay, 1946, p. 207.
2. *Ibid.,* p. 208.
3. Thus spoke Ambedkar, *op. cit.,* p. 8.
4. Dhananjey Keer, *Dr. Ambedkar: His life and Mission,* Popular Prakashan, Bombay, 1962, p. 327.
5. B. R. Ambedkar, *What Congress and Gandhi Have done to the Untouchables.* Thackers & Co. Ltd. Bombay, 1945, p. 204.
6. Speech delivered by Ambedkar in the Constituent Assembly, New Delhi on 17-12-1946.
7. Thus Spoke Ambedkar, *op. cit.,* pp. 97-98.
8. *Ibid.,* p. 98.
9. B.R. Ambedkar, *Pakistan or the Partition of India, op. cit.,* pp. 180-81.
10. *Ibid.,* p. 13.
11. *Ibid.*
12. Jawaharlal Nehru, *The Discovery of India, op. cit.,* p. 340.
13. B. R. Ambedkar, *Pakistan or the Partition of India, op. cit.,* p. 21.
14. *Ibid.,* p. 259.
15. *Ibid.,* p. 185.
16. *Ibid.,* p. 322.
17. *Ibid.,* p. 331.
18. *Ibid.*
19. *Ibid.,* p. 344.
20. B. R. Ambedkar, *Thoughts of Linguistic States,* Ramkrishna Printing Press, Bombay, 1955, p. 12.
21. *Ibid.*
22. B.R. Ambedkar, *Annihilation of Caste,* Katra Jaman Sangh, Amritsar, 1944, p. 37.
23. B.R. Ambedkar, *States and Minorities,* Thakcer & Co. Ltd., Bombay, 1947, p. 52.
24. E. Barker, *Principles of Social and Political Theory, op. cit.,* p. 161
25. Round Table Conference Proceedings, pp. 438-41.
26. B.R. Ambedkar, *Pakistan or the Partition of India, op. cit.,* p. 261.
27. *Ibid.,* p. 383
28. *Ibid.,* p. 371
29. Dhananjay Keer: *Dr. Ambedkar, His Life and Mission, op. cit.,* p. 234.
30. B. R. Ambedkar, *Ranade, Gandhi and Jinnah, op. cit.,* pp. 48-49.
31. *Ibid.,* p. 59.

4

AMBEDKAR ON PHILOSOPHY

Ambedkar strives for a balance between thought and action and he endeavoured to maintain it earnestly. His life has been a life of purpose and principle. His political philosophy grows out of his unbending struggle for the freedom of the servile humanity. His moral stamina cannot tolerate the unjust environment which has been arresting the movement of social progress and holding humanity in fetters, for centuries past. He holds that man should not conserve the whole of his social heritage, but select what is helpful and transmit to future generations only that much and no more. His principle of dynamism recognises that there is nothing fixed, nothing eternal, nothing *sanatan,* that everything is changing, that change is the law of life for individuals as well as for society. His humanism stands for radical change for the material and spiritual good of man and society.

Ambedkar was highly influenced by the humanistic outlook and liberal attitude of his teacher, Prof. Dewey, He said, "Prof. John Dewey, who was my teacher and to whom I owe so much, has said: Every society gets encumbered with what is trivial, with dead wood from the past, and with what is perverse . . . As a society becomes more englightened, it realises that it is responsible not to conserve and transmit the whole of its existing achievements, but only such as make for a better future society."[1] His philosophical approach is a kind of indifference to epistomology, however, with serious consideration for metaphysical problems.

Ambedkar does not take any interest in the affairs of other worldliness. But he attaches more importance to the illumination of human purposes and the coordination and elevation of human life. Things must be measured by their standards of survival value. He does not attach more importance to differences, natural and necessary, but to the best elements in human life, which have survived for the betterment of human society. He said, "whether it is sufficient to take the placed view of the anthropologist that there is nothing to be said about the beliefs, habits, morals and outlooks on life, which obtain among the different peoples of the world except that they often differ; or whether it is not necessary to make an attempt to find out what kind of morality, beliefs, habits and outlook have worked best and have enabled those who possessed them to flourish, to go strong, to people and earth and to have dominion over it".[2]

Ambedkar wants every society to have a workable scheme of human life. A society should have practical morality and social religion. Every man should have a philosophy of life, for everyone must have a standard by which to measure his conduct. And philosphy is nothing but a standard by which to measure. Men should have certain principles of human living according to which they should channelise their thoughts and actions in such a way that all may feel real happiness.

Ambedkar has undying faith in the essential goodness of man and the vast potentiality that is in him. He knows from history that injustice is not removed till the sufferer himself does away with it by his own exertions and exhibitions. He always believes in self-help. He does not aspire for any extra-mundane help for the mitigation of human suffering. He said, "You had better die and relieve this world if you cannot rise to a new life and if you cannot rejuvenate yourselves. As a matter of fact it is your birthright to get food, shelter and clothing in this land in equal proportion with every individual high or low. If you believe in living a respectable life, you believe in self-help which is the best help".[3]

Ambedkar does not believe in the permanent soul residing inside human body. To him, the soul is merely an speculation. The discussion of the existence of the soul is as unfruitful as the discussion of the existence of God. The belief in soul is far more dangerous than the belief in God. He condemns the practice of priesthood. He believes only in human consciousness. In his scheme of life, there is no soul, no God to govern the life of man. He rules out the possibility of the past *Karmas* done in previous lives as the regulator of human existence. There is an extended doctrine of past *karmas,* which he opposes root and branch. He said, "The basis of the Hindu doctrine of past Karma as the regulator of future life is an iniquitous doctrine. What could have been the purpose of inventing such a doctrine? The only purpose one can think of is to enable the state or the society to escape responsibility for the conditions of the poor and the lowly".[4]

Ambedkar is not interested in enjoying the life of *heaven* for the present suffering. He believes in the present life and cares little for what happens after death. He adheres to the principle of understanding rather than the rejection of life. He stands for the improvement of life and not for the destruction of it. To him, the law of past actions as formulated in the Hindu way of life, saps completely the spirit of revolt. He seeks to find in positivism a basics for a social reconstruction, which can elevate human life to a better standard and establish a religion of humanity.

Ambedkar looks towards man with great regard and respect. He wants every man to live a dignified life. He said, "It is graceful to live at the cost of one's self-respect. Self-respect is a most vital factor in life. Without it, man is a mere cipher. To live worthily with self-respect one has to overcome difficulties. It is out of hard and ceaseless struggle alone that one derives strength, confidence and recognition."[5] An honourable life is always a dignified life. He does not see any novelty in mere survivalness, if devoid of a high standard of culture. He said, "There are different modes of survival. But all are not equally honourable. For an individual as well as for a society, there is a gulf between merely living and living worthily. To fight in a battle and to live in glory is one mode. To beat a retreat, to surrender and to live the life of a captive is also a mode of survival".[6] What he wants is not the mere survival but a life of respect, of justice and equality.

Ambedkar agrees with Modern Science which has shown that lumping together of individuals into a few sharply marked-off classes is a superficial view of man noteworthy of serious consideration. Consequently, the utilisation of the qualities of individuals is incompatible with their stratification by classes, since the qualitieis of individuals are so variable. He does not accept Plato's concept of man. What attracts him in man is his uniqueness, his ability, courage and reflective thought in the times of calamity and crisis, though man's life is not generally so. He holds that man's life is a continual change an interesting adventure, a mission of tide and fortune. He said, "Man's life is generally habitual and unreflective. Reflective thought, in the sense of active, persistent and careful consideration of any belief or supposed form or knowledge in the light of the grounds that support it and further conclusions to which it tends, is quite rare and arises only in a situation which presents a dilemma—a crisis".[7]

Ambedkar has an immense faith in man and with such a faith in the strength of man, he wants man to be devoted to the service of humanity. He said, "Life can be ennobled and immortalised by sacrificing it for lasting good such as the cause of truth, a vow, honour or country. For the protection of human rights several great men have immolated themselves at the altar of duty. Better to die in the prime of youth for a great cause than to live like an oak and do nothing".[8] He finds in man something that offers society prosperity or elevation in this world. He regards and attaches more importance to a life of devotion. It is the only life worth living. Man should not be without a mission.

Ambedkar does not believe in any *Divine Dispensation* for the emancipation of mankind and the welfare of society. He said,

"A man is great because he finds a way to save society in its hour of crisis. But what can help him to find the way? He can do so only with the help of intellect. Intellect is the light. Nothing else can be of any avail . . . that without the combination of sincerity and intellect no man can be great".[9] He wants something more to be done by a Great man to the society in which he has to live. Eminence and greatness are two different things and, therefore, a great man must have something more than what merely an eminent individual has. A great man should be a great social reformer and his whole life should be nothing but a relentless campaign for social reform.

A great man faces a challenge from traditional societies, though he himself is a challenge to them. Ambedkar said, "Most people do not realise that society can practise tyranny and oppression against an individual in a far greater degree than a Government can. The means and scope that are open to society for oppression are more extensive than those that are open to Government, also they are far more effective."[10] To him a *Social Reformer* is more courageous than a Political Patriot. He said, "when the Social Reformer challenges society there is nobody to hail him a martyr. There is nobody even to befriend him. He is loathed and shunned. But when the political patriot challenges Government he has whole society to support him. He is praised, admired and elevated as the saviour. Who shows more courage—The Social Reformer who fights alone or the Political Patriot who fights under the cover of vast mass of supporters?'[11]

Ambedkar has a deep faith in man and his powers. To him, man is something more than God. He does not believe in God. He said, "You must abolish your slavery yourself. Do not depend for its abolition upon God or *Superman*. Your salvation lies in *political powers* and not in making pilgrimages and observance of fasts. Devotion to scriptures would not free you from your bondage, want and poverty. Your forefathers have been doing it for generations, but there has been no respite nor even a slight difference in your miserable life in any way. Like your forefathers, you wear rags. Like them, you subsist on thrown-out crumbs; like them, you perish in utter slums and hovels; and like them, you fall easy victims to diseases with a death-rate that rages among poultry. Your religious fasts, austerities and penances have not saved you from starvation."[12] He opposes the spiritualistic fads and superstitions of the people, which have emasculated and devitalised them for many years past.

Ambedkar rejects belief in the existence of God on rational and empirical grounds. The belief in God gives rise to belief in the efficacy of worship and prayer and the efficacy of worship and prayer gives rise to the office of the priest and the priest is the evil genious who creates all superstitions and thereby destroys the growth of right view. The belief in

God is unprofitable both from individual and social point of view, for such a belief makes man inactive, dormant, fatalist, and indifferent to the woes of mankind. He said, "The appearance of *Tulsi* leaves around your neck will not relieve you from the cluthces of the money-lenders. Because you sing songs of *Rama,* you will not get a concession in rent from the landlords. You will not get salaries at the end of the month because you make pilgrimages every year to Pandharpur. Because the major part of the society is absorbed in these worthless mysteries of life, superstitions and mysticism, the intelligent and self-centred people get ample scope and opportunities to carry out their anti-social designs'.[13] He englightens the people to understand their own affairs themselves.

Ambedkar does not teach the people to adopt wrong means to end their miseries of life. He said, "Give up eating carrion. People ask me then what they should eat. In reply, I ask you to remember the example of a virtuous woman. She will never accept the life of a prostitute for betterment though she falls on evil days. She suffers for self-respect. Learn to live in this world with respect. You should always cherish some ambition to do some thing in this world. They alone rise who strive. Some of you nurse the wrong notion that you will not rise in this world. But remember that the age of helplessness in ended. A new epoch has set in".[14] He instils strong optimistic values in the minds of the people. He does not believe in *avatarvada.* To him, the *avatar* theory does not require that God should be pure in his making. All that the Brahmanic theory of *Avatar* says is that God saves his followers by taking different forms although God may be very impure and immoral in his conduct.

Ambedkar accepts that the centre of religion should not be between man and God, but between man and man. To him, the purpose of religion should be to teach man how he should be towards other man so that all may be happy. Regarding his attitude towards God, he said, "If the so-called God has created something out of something, then that something, out of which something new was created has been in existence before he created anything. God cannot, therefore, be called the Creator of that something which has existed before Him. If something has been created by somebody out of something before God created anything, than God cannot be said to be the Creator or the first cause."[15] The belief in God or supernatural being is a belief in falsehood to him.

Ambedkar comes very near to the naturalistic view of life. Human life is closely related with nature. He holds that every event has a cause, though the cause is the result of some human action or natural law. He believes in the free nature of man. He said, "Every event must be the result of man's action or of an act of Nature. There cannot be any event which is supernatural in its origin. It may be that man is not able to discover the real cause of the occurrence of an event. But if he has intelligence, he is bound one day to discover it."[16] He has three objects in his mind-to lead man to the path of rationalism, to free man to go in search of truth and to remove the most potent source of superstition. His naturalistic attitude regards man as a part of Nature. He does not want man to depend upon any supernatural factor, because it leads man to a lose of self-reliance, courage and confidence.

According to Ambedkar, *religion* means the life-breath for man and society. It is the essence of human wisdom. It is a driving force for human society. He does not regard religion as worthless. He stands as an ardent advocate for the need of religion in human relations. Religion is a part of one's social inheritance and the life of the individual and society are bound up with it. It is very difficult to abandon it. He is opposed to an organised and wrongly institutionalised religion. He said, "The religion which discriminates between two followers is partial and the religion which treats crores of its adherents worse than dogs and criminals and inflicts upon them insufferable disabilities is no religion at all. Religion is not the appellation for such an unjust order. Religion and slavery are incompatible."[17]

Religion is for the service of man and not man, as a means, to religion. Ambedkar said, "The religion that does not teach its followers to show humanity in dealing with its coreligionists is nothing but a display of force. The religion that asks it adherents to suffer the touch of animals but not the touch of human beings is not religion but a mockery. That religion which precludes some classes from education, forbids them to accumulate wealth and to bear arms, is not religion but a mockery. The religion that compels the ignorant to be ignorant and the poor to be poor, is not religion but a visitation.'[18] He does not want any type of hypocrisy, injustice and exploitation of man by man. He links religion with the social well-being of the people. He does not reduce religion to merely a means to organic needs of man. He gives it a higher and respectable place with reference to economic elements in human life. Religion, social status and property are all sources of power and authority to him.

Ambedkar does not believe in a religion of Rules and Laws, but only in a religion of principles. He said, "Rules are practical; they are habitual ways of doing things according to prescription. But principles are intellectual. they are useful methods of judging things. Rules seeks to tell an agent just what course of action to pursue. Principles do not prescribe a specific course of action. Rules, like cooking recipes, do tell just what to do and how to do it. A principle, such as that of justice, supplies a main head by reference to which he is to consider the bearings of his desires and purposes, it guides him in his thinking by suggesting to him the important consideration which he should bear in mind."[19] To him, doing good by virtue of a rule and doing good in the light of a principle are two different things. He said, "The principle may be wrong but the act is conscious and responsible. The rule may be right but the act is mechanical. A religious act may not be a correct act but at least it must be a responsible act. To allow this responsibility, religion must mainly be a matter of principles only. It cannot be a matter of rules. The moment it degenerates into rules it cease to be Religion, as it kills responsibility which is the essence of a truly religious act."[20] He looks towards a religion as a source of social and spiritual unity.

According to Ambedkar, there are four characteristics of a true religion. They are:

(1) That society must have either the sanction of law or the sanction of morality to hold it together. Without either, society is sure to go to pieces.
(2) Religion must be in accord with science.
(3) Religion must recognise the fundamental tenets of liberty, equality and fraternity.
(4) Religion must not sanctify or ennable poverty. His religious attitude oppose superstition, idolatry, dogmatism, hypocrisy, sectarianism, fanaticism, individualism, mysticism and conventionalism, poverty and ignorance, in religion. He stands for a religion which is democratic out and out. The foundation of his religion is his faith in the capacities of human nature, faith in human intelligence and equality.

Ambedkar's concept of religion is purely anthropocentric. It is secular and not extra-mundane. A religion that disintegrates the human society is not a true religion. It is a rational one, a moral one, and a spiritual one. He regards *Dhamma* as religion. *Dhamma* differ from what is called Religion. He said, "Religion, it is said, is personal and one must keep it to oneself. One must not let it play its part in public life. Contrary to this, Dhamma is social. It is fundamentally and essentially so." His view of religion is social and secular and morality is the keynote of it. *Dhamma* is righteousness, which means right relations between man and man in all spheres of life. Right relations have to be established on the basis of social principles of liberty, equality and fraternity.

Morality is the soul of what Ambedkar regards Dhamma as religion. He said, "Morality arises from the direct necessity for man to love man. It does not require the sanction of God. It is not to please God that man has to be moral. It is for his own good that man has to love man."[21] Dhamma as religion rejects belief in God, belief in soul, worship of God, curing of the erring soul, propitiating God by prayers, ceremonies, sacrifices, etc. He regards Buddha's *Dhamma* as true religion the purpose of which is to reconstruct the world by establishing right relations among human beings. A well-ordered society is the central theme of his concept of religion.

Ambedkar is not against the very existence of *Hinduism* and Hindu leaders but he is dead pitched against its wrong ideals and the tenacity of Hindu leaders to them. He said, "If I am disgusted with Hindus and Hinduism, it is because I am convinced that they cherish wrong ideals and live a wrong social life. My quarrel with Hindus and Hinduism is not over the imperfection of their social conduct. It is much more fundamental. It is over their ideals."[22] The reason of dissatisfaction lies in the fact that Hinduism gives no support to social unity. He said, "Hinduism and social union are incompatible. By its very genius Hinduism believes in social separation which is another name for social disunity and even creates social separation. If the Hindus wish to be one they will have to discard Hinduism. They cannot be one without violating Hinduism. Hinduism—the traditional social structure-is the greatest obstacle to Hindu unity. Hinduism cannot create that longing to belong which is the basis of social unity. On the contrary, Hinduism creates an eagerness to separate."[23]

Ambedkar is a revolt against all that is *evil* and an obstacle to social unity and human progress. He accepts that Hinduism was once a missionary religion. It is wrong to thing that he is for the destruction of Hinduism. His main concern is to reform and reconstruct it. He said, "Whether you do that or you do not, you must give a new doctrinal basis to your Religion—a basis that will be in consonance with *Liberty. Equality* and *Fraternity,* in short with Democracy. I am no authority on the subject. But I am told that for such religious principles as will be in consonance with Liberty, Equality and Fraternity it may not be necessary for you to borrow from foreign sources and that you could draw for such principles on the *Upanishadas.*"[24] The Hindu society should be re-organised on two main principles—equality and absence of castcism.

Ambedkar wishes man not only to have inner perfection but also external adjustment. The combination of both can help man and his society to make themselves whole, harmonious and illumined one. He said, "If the *Brahmin* pervades all, a *Brahmin* and an *Untouchable* are equal. But the people do not apply the doctrine to social organisation and keep the discussion on a vedantic level. Had they applied it on a social level and preached social equality, their vedantic gospel would have been profound and worth consideration, apart from its erroneous belief that the world is an illusion."[25]

According to Ambedkar, society is an organisation based on some human attitudes. He said, "Men do not become a society by living in physical proximity any more than a man ceases to be a member of his society by living so many miles away from other men . . . similarity in habits, customs, beliefs and thoughts, is not enough to constitute men into society. Things may be passed physically from one to another like bricks. In the same way, habits and customs, beliefs and thoughts of one group may be taken over by another group and there may thus appear a similarity between the two."[26] What he wants is not merely a sense of similarity but also an ardent faith in the common unity of purpose among the different members of a society.

According to Ambedkar, "Men constitute a society because they have things which they possess in common. To have similar things is totally different from possessing things in common. And the only way by which men can come to possess things in common with one another is by being in communication with one another. This is merely another way of saying that *Society* continues to exist by communication, indeed in communication."[27] In fact, *communication* brings a certain like mindedness in the people and a certain recognition that their good is a common one. He holds that making the individual a sharer or partner in the associated activity so that he feels its success as his success, its failure as his failure is the real thing that binds men and makes a society of them.

According to Ambedkar, the caste system prevents common activity and by preventing common activity it has prevented the Hindus from becoming a society with a unified life and a consciousness of its own being. The real basis of a society lies in a unified feeling and common activity. He conceives a society based upon a clear consciousness of things to be pursued that are in some degree, for the benefit of all individuals. In any social organisation, no part should be ignored.

Ambedkar discards unnecessary and unatural and menacing disparity which obstructs social progress, and also results in the unnecessary balkanisation of the society. Social *stability* depends upon the best social adjustment among the different social units. The canons of social adjustment are fluidity and equity. He said, "One thing nobody wants is a static relationship, something that is unalternable, something that is fixed for all times. *Stability* is wanted but not at the cost of change when change is imperative. Second thing nobody wants is mere adjustment. *Adjustment* is wanted but not at the sacrifice of social justice."[28] Social stability depends upon the attitude of men who constitute society. So long as there is a caste system, the idea of social solidarity and unity is remote. He does not agree with the Arya Samaj and its ideology which has obstructed social stability and has created a sense of social stagnation.

Ambedkar holds that man in circumstances is wholly responsible for present *poverty* and suffering. The present suffering is due to man's own activities done in this life. He holds that the fate of the individual is governed by his environment and the circumstances he is obliged to live under, and if an individual is suffering from want and misery it is because his environment is not propitious. The social organisation may be held responsible for the state of society and the status of man. Inequity, exploitation, tyranny, coercion, hatred, greed and lust, all are a negation of an ideal social relationship. He is vehemently opposed to wrong ideals. He condemns a society based on dual standards, which make a false basis of social organisation. He said, "I realise that the world is very imperfect and any one who wants to live in it must bear with it imperfections. But while I am prepared to bear with the imperfections and shortcomings of the society in which I may be destined to labour, I feel I should not consent to live in a society which cherishes wrong ideals or a society which having right ideals will not consent to bring its social life in conformity with those ideals".[29]

According to Ambedkar, an *ideal society* should be mobile, should be full of channels for conveying a change taking place in one part to other parts. In an ideal society there should be many interests consciously communicated and shared. There should be varied and free points of contact with other modes of association. His view of society includes equality, freedom, love, democracy, brotherhood and communication. The soul of his ideal society is social conscience, without which no ideal society can exist on earth. He believes that social conscience cannot accept wrong relationship. He said, "No society with a social conscience has ever accepted . . . inequity on the ground that whatever is once settled is settled for all times. Such a view is opposed to all morality . . . On the contrary, whatever progress in improving the terms of associated life between individuals and classes has been made in the course of history, is due entirely to the recognition of the ethical doctrine that what is wrongly settled is never settled and must be re-settled."[30] Social conscience with its corresponding ideals of liberty, equality and fraternity, constitutes the real basis of an ideal living in his political thought.

Ambedkar created *human rights* equally for both men and women. He wants that women should not lag behind in the activities of social reform. He is a great believer in women's progress and organisation. He measures the progress of a community and a society by the degree of progress which women achieve. He advised the women in India. He said, "(1) Learn to be clean, (2) Keep away from vices, (3) Give education to your children, (4) Remove from them all inferiority complex, (5) Instil ambition into them, (6) Inculcate in their minds that they are destined to be great, and (7) Do not be in a hurry to marry".[31] He holds that marriage is a liability. He said, "The parental duty lies in giving each child a better start than its parents had. Above all, let every girl who marries, stand by her husband, claim to be her husband's friend and equal, and refuse to be his slave. I am sure if you follow this advice, you will bring honour and glory to yourselves".[32]

Ambedkar stresses the need of the cultivation of the mind and the spirit of self-help among the men and women. He wants them to realise that they owe a great responsibility for educating their children in right way. To him, education is the most important factor for moulding the life of all men, women and children. He wants to make not only men but also women bold and fearless, courageous and intelligent, so that they can manage many of their affairs themselves in their homes and in their communities. He said, "Never regard yourself as untouchables. Live a clean life. Dress yourself like the touchable ladies, never mind if your dress is full of patches, but see that it is clean. None can restrict your freedom in the choice of your garments and in the use of the metal for your ornaments."[33]

Ambedkar was not only a progressive and social humanist, but also a *genius.* He stood and spoke for the cause of the suppressed humanity. He demanded freedom and equality for all men and women. He revived the perennial philosophy of Buddha, for the emancipation of ignored humanity. He was not only a learned man, but also an intellectual, who sacrificed his life for the dignity and uplift of the poorest of the poor of the world.

Ambedkar consciously or unconsciously directed his humanism against orthodoxies and wrong traditions of man and society, which aimed to dehumanise, to subordinate the very existence of human beings. His philosophical thought attaches great importance to man. His social humanism does not believe in the absoluteness of values. It believes in social relativism. His humanistic philosophy is practical and pragmatic, social and moral, definite and dynamic, individualistic and socialistic. He attempts at a harmony between men and society.

REFERENCES

1. B.R. Ambedkar, *Annihilation of Caste,* Katra Jaman Sangh, Amritsar, 1944. p. 78.
2. *Ibid.*, p. 77.
3. Dhananjay Keer, *Dr. Ambedkar: His Life and Mission,* Popular Prakashan, Bombay, 1962, pp. 60-61.
4. B. R. Ambedkar, *The Buddha and His Dhamma,* People's Education Society, Bombay, 1957, p. 344.
5. Dhananjay Keer, *Dr. Ambedkar: His Life and Mission, op.cit.,* p. 127.
6. B.R. Ambedkar, *Annihilation of Caste, op. cit.,* p. 55.

7. *Ibid.*, p. 68.
8. Dhananjay Keer, *Dr. Ambedkar: His Life and Mission, op. cit.*, pp. 91-92.
9. *B.R. Ambedkar, Ranade, Gandhi and Jinnah, op. cit.*, p. 13.
10. *Ibid.*, p. 21.
11. *Ibid.*, p. 22.
12. Dhananjay Keer, *Dr. Ambedkar: His Life and Mission, op. cit.*, p. 234.
13. *Ibid.*, p. 218.
14. *Ibid.*, p. 233.
15. *B. R. Ambedkar, The Buddha and His Dhamma, op. cit.*, p. 255.
16. *Ibid.*, p. 250.
17. Dhananjay Keer, *Dr. Ambedkar: His Life and Mission, op. cit.*, p. 92.
18. *Ibid.*, pp. 273-74.
19. B. R. Ambedkar, *Annihilation of Caste, op. cit.*, p. 71.
20. *Ibid.*
21. B. R. Ambedkar, *The Buddha and His Dhamma, op. cit.*, p. 323.
22. B. R. Ambedkar, *Annihilation of Caste, op. cit.*, p. 26.
23. B.R. Ambedkar, *What Congress and Gandhi have done to the Untouchables*, Thacker & Co. Ltd., Bombay, 1945, p. 187.
24. B. R. Ambedkar, *Annihilation of Caste, op. cit.*, p. 76.
25. Dhananjay Keer, *Dr. Ambedkar: His Life and Mission, op. cit.*, p. 506.
26. B. R. Ambedkar, *Annihilation of Caste, op. cit.*, pp. 26-27.
27. *Ibid.*, p. 27.
28. *Ibid.*, Appendix II, p. 21.
29. *Ibid.*, Appendix II, pp. 25-26.
30. B. R. Ambedkar, *Who Were the Shudras?* Thacker & Co., Ltd. Bombay, 1946, p. 15.
31. Dhananjay Keer, *Dr. Ambedkar: His Life and Mission, op. cit.*, p. 350.
32. *Ibid.*
33. *Ibid.*, pp. 104-05.

5

AMBEDKAR ON SOCIETY AND SOCIALISM

Man needs leisure for the cultivation of mind and the pursuit of a full human life. If he is to be a good citizen, he must have some leisure for his general civic obligations and for the development of his own personality, as well as for the exercise of his special function. This involves the recognition that some limitation should be put to the time that is devoted to labour, and this is one of the things that it may be necessary to secure by some form of central control. Ambedkar holds that the State must take some responsibility for running industries. Key industries should be owned and run by the state and even industries which are not key industries but are basic industries should also be owned by the state. In doing so, the economic exploitation of the people may be minimised. The primary function of a growing society is an effective check on economic exploitation.

Ambedkar's ideal of *socialism* can be achieved only when there are people in power who govern honestly and are sincerely devoted to the task of socialism. The power of the state should not go to those people who are opposed to socialist ideas. All things in a democratic society, depend on the wishes of the people. It is up to them whether to choose or not to choose a particular section of representatives. State power is an important factor in man's progress. He said, "The main purpose behind the *State Control* is to put an obligation on the state to plan the economic life of the people on lines which would lead to highest point of productivity without closing every avenue to private enterprise, and also provide for the equitable distribution of wealth".[1]

Ambedkar seeks state control not only to avoid the waste of *capitalism* but also to enable it to work on socialist lines. He remains an opponent of *communism*. He does not accept the Marxian solution that the right to private property be abolished for the well-being of the poor classes. What he wants is that the state should peacefully and legally, remove social, political and economic inequality by providing better opportunities to the submerged classes and make it possible for every subject to enjoy freedom from want and freedom fear. He is very critical of capitalism which has no sympathy for the needy and the weak. He desires drastic changes in the attitude of capitalism. He is fundamentally an individualist—socialist in his economic and social philosophy.

To Ambedkar, guild socialism, syndicalism, Christian socialism, fabian socialism and scientific socialism are not very convincing. He accepts the theory of state socialism with necessary changes. State intervention is essential for economic efficiency when and where the public interest is neglected. As he believes in the individual liberty, he does not want to annihilate the capitalists. He wishes them to give place to a better and a saner ordering of economic and social affairs. He proposes state socialism. He said, "*State socialism* is essential for the rapid *industrialisation* of India. Private enterprise cannot do it and if it did it would produce those inequalities of wealth which private capitalism has produced in Europe and which should be a warning to Indians."[2] The plan set out in his theory of state socialism proposes state ownership in agriculture with a collectivised method of cultivation and a modified form of state socialism in the field of industry.

Ambedkar proposes the nationalisation of insurance companies. He said, "Nationalised Insurance gives the individual greater security than the private firm does in as much as it pledges the resources of the state as a security for the ultimate payment of his insurance money. It also gives the state the resources necessary for financing its economic planning in the absence of which it would have to resort to borrowing from the money market at a high rate of interest."[3] He defends man's right to private possession and property. He stands for a greater security of the individual's economic interests with the help of state control.

Ambedkar agrees with State socialist who raises the lower strata of the working classes at the expense of the higher classes and puts a check upon the excessive accumulation of wealth among certain strata of society and certain members of the propertied classes. He does not agree with state socialists like Rodbertus and Lassale on the questions of capitalist system and private property. He gives way to individual incentive for the economic well-being of the people. He is firmly convinced of the indispensability of the industrialisation of India through both key and basic industries. He does not want the concentration of wealth in a few hands. He was not only convinced that planned economy was essential for reaping the full fruits of industrialisation, but he also believed in its rapid and firm success. In his socialism, there exists a moral solidarity which is much more fundamental than any economic tie between the various individuals and classes of this great nation.

Ambedkar fought against tyranny, injustice and false traditions in order to release the suffering people from bondage. He knew well that the results and effects of poverty upon the people were intolerable. *Poverty* is the greatest enemy of his political ideas. He was intensely moved by the inhuman conditions of his suppressed community. He built his personality on patient labour, burning sincerity, supreme courage and selfless sacrifice. He struggled against injustice, social slavery, inequality and poverty. He is a combination of both love and hate love for knowledge and hate for ignorance and poverty.

Ambedkar condemns everything extols poverty. His idea of socialism is an attack on *poverty,* because poverty is responsible for diseased bodies and frustrated lives. He does not agree with those men who develop a sort of stoic endurance and resignation towards poverty. To him, poverty and *socialism* cannot exist together. His concept of socialism does not stand for equality of identity. His socialism recognises human distinctions based on merit. Its chief aim is to remove the extreme inequalities. His concept of socialism is based on the principles of justice and right.

Ambedkar does not wish to leave the establishment of state socialism to the will of the Legislature. He wants that the economic structure of society should be prescribed by Constitutional Law. He said, "the purpose is to protect the liberty of the individual from invasion by other individuals which is the object of enacting *Fundamental Rights.* The connection between individual liberty and the shape and form of the economic structure of society may not be apparent to everyone. Nonetheless the connection between the two is real."[4] The fundamental rights have no value to unemployed persons. He said, "The fear of starvation, the fear of losing a house, the fear of losing savings, if any, the fear of having to be a burden on public charity, the fear of having to be burned or buried at public cost are factors two strong to permit a man to stand out for his fundamental rights. The unemployed are, thus, compelled to relinquish their fundamental rights for the sake of securing the privilege to work and to subsist."[5]

Ambedkar favours the protection of employed as well as unemployed persons. He wants that they should not be coerced and cheated out of their fundamental rights to life, liberty and pursuit of happiness. One of the remedies adopted by Democratic countries is to limit the power of Government to impose arbitrary restraints in political domain and to invoke the ordinary power of the legislature to restrain the more powerful individual from imposing arbitrary restraints on the less powerful in the economic field. But he does not accept it as quite practicable. He said, "The successful invocation by the less powerful of the authority of the Legislature is a doubtful proposition. Having regard to the fact that even under adult suffrage all legislatures and Governments are controlled by the more powerful, an appeal to the Legislature to intervene is a very precarious safeguard against the invasion of the liberty of the less powerful."[6]

Ambedkar's method seeks to limit not only the power of Government to impose arbitrary restraints but also of the more powerful individuals or to be more precise to eliminate the possibility of the more powerful having the power to impose arbitrary restraints on the less powerful by withdrawing from the control he has over the economic life of the people. His proposal is essentially a faith for safeguarding the liberty of the individual under the socialist pattern of society. To him, *individualism* and *socialism* do not appear as inherently contradictory. He carefully relates his socialist ideas to the idea of parliamentary democracy, free thought and expression. He is an individualist by his temperament and training, and at the same time, he is a socialist by his intelligence and intellect. His concept of state socialism liberates people from the capitalist's coercion and threats and ensures an equitable distribution of material wealth. His socialism does not restrict man's free choice of living and movement in society. He does not believe that the state crushes the individuality of the individuals.

Ambedkar is very critical of the Indian socialist programme which is unrelated to the social needs of the people. He admits that there cannot be ultimate equality among the people so long as men differ in their needs and capacities. He would certainly agree with Prof. Laski that equality implies fundamentally a certain levelling process. His love for equality is a process of levelling and in includes the absence of special privileges and provisions for adequate opportunities to all. He said, "A statesman is concerned with vast numbers of people. He has neither the time nor the knowledge to draw fine distinctions and to treat each equitably, i.e., according to need or according to capacity. However, desirable or reasonable an equitable treatment of men may be, humanity is not capable of assortment and classification. The statesman, therefore, must follow some rough and ready rule and that rough and rule is to treat all men alike not because they are alike but because classification and assortment is impossible."[7] His love for equality and hate for inequality, ignorance and poverty, constitute the basic attitude towards a socialist spirit.

Socialism is a problem of social war. Ambedkar said, "Social war has been raging between the strong and the weak for more violently in Europe than it has been in India. Yet the weak in Europe has had in freedom of military service his physical weapon, in suffrage his political weapon and in education his moral weapon. These three weapons for emancipation were never withheld by the strong from the weak in Europe.

All these weapons were, however, denied to the masses in India by *Chaturvarnya*".[8] The Hindu social theory of *Chaturvarnya* divides men into four classes and it denies the *shudras* the right to education, arms and property. This system prevented the people from rising to either socialism or to capitalism. He said, "The caste system is a system which is infested with the spirit of isolation and in fact, it makes isolation of one caste from another a matter of virtue".[9] This spirit of *isolationism* is the chief hurdle in the way of socialism.

In Ambedkar's ideal social organisation men would bot be forced to do particular work. They would be free to choose and to work. This would definitely increase their economic efficiency and strengthen the prospects of democracy and socialism. He regards division of labour as an indispensable condition for greater economic efficiency. Civilised society undoubtedly needs division of labour. Division of labour is simply the spontaneous realisation of a particular form of social cooperation. This division of labour effects an easy and natural combination of economic efforts for the creation of material dividend. The caste system is not merely a division of labour, but also a division of labourers. He said, "This division of labour is not spontaneous, it is not based on natural aptitudes. Social and individual efficiency requires us to develop the capacity of an individual to the point of competency to choose and to make his own career. This principle is violated in the caste system in so far as it involves an attempt to appoint tasks to individuals in advance, selected not on the basis of trained original capacities, but on that of the social status of parents".[10]

According to Ambedkar, "Industry is never static. It undergoes rapid and abrupt changes. With such changes an individual must be free to change his occupation. Without such freedom to adjust himself to changing circumstances it would be impossible for him to gain his livelihood."[11] The social organisation based on *Chaturvarnya* diverts the minds of the people from greater economic efficiency which is required in the successful working of socialism. It compels people to do hereditary professions, though they are not prepared to do them. The social theory of *Vedanta* is an anti-thesis of socialism. Socialism teaches social equality and human brotherhood, whereas the *Varna* system creates social inequality.

Modern technology and civilisation have produced some social and economic evils. Ambedkar said, "If machinery and civilisation have not benefited everybody, the remedy is not to condemn machinery and civilisation but to alter the organisation of society so that the benefits will not be usurped by the few but will accrue to all".[12] He has a deep faith in man. He does not regard him merely as an animal. Man shares the constitutions and functions of animals, yet these are not his distinctively human functions. In his idea of socialism, man occupies the highest place in the scheme of animate existence. Man's aim should be something cultural along with material well-being. What divides the man from the brute is culture. He said, "Culture is not possible for the brute, but it is essential for man. That being so, the aim of human society must be to enable every person to lead a life of culture, which means the cultivation of mind as distinguished from the satisfaction of mere physical wants".[13]

According to Ambedkar, *leisure* means the lessening of the toil and effort necessary for satisfying the physical wants of life. The most urgent need that socialism has to face here in this country, is how to provide leisure to individual. He said, "It is possible only when machine takes the place of man. There is no other means of producing leisure. *Machinery* and modern civilisation are, thus, indispensable for emancipating man from leading the life of a brute, and for providing him with leisure and for making a life of culture possible".[14] He relates his concept of socialism with the utility of modern machines. He does not undermine the need of a democratic society with its ideal of socialism. A democratic society, so organised, would not be indifferent to modern machine and civilisation. To him, a democratic society must assure a life of leisure and culture to each one of its citizen. This is a genuine step towards socialism.

Once Mr. Nehru remarked that it is technology not ideology, which can enhance the cause of human progress. But to Ambedkar, both technology and ideology are essential, if man is to make human society a place of material well-being and a home for spiritual brotherhood. Technology without ideology is blind and ideology without technology is empty in modern society. In his socialism, the common man is not to be compelled to work ceaselessly for a pittance and remain like a brute.

Ambedkar sincerely associates his idea of socialism with democracy in order to foster and promote the common economic, intellectual and moral interests of the people. Parliamentary democracy is unsuited for bringing about *State socialism. Dictatorship* then remains as an alternative. It can give the permanences which state socialism requires as an essential condition for its fruitification. So, a dilemma arises. The problem is to have state socialism without dictatorship or to have state socialism with *parliamentary democracy.* He said, "The wayout seems to retain Parliamentary Democracy and to prescribe state socialism by the law of the Constitution so that it will be beyond the reach of a parliamentary majority to suspend, amend or abrogate it. It is only by this that one can achieve the triple object, namely, to establish socialism, retain parliamentary democracy and avoid *Dictatorship".*[15]

Ambedkar's theory of *State socialism* marks a departure from the existing Constitutions of democratic countries. He stands for both democracy and socialism and endeavours to avoid dictatorship. He is a strong supporter of Lockean political and economic liberalism. The link between democracy and socialism is the most important element in his thought. He wants individual freedom through democracy and social welfare through socialism. Social welfare without individual liberty is a coercion and individual liberty without aiming at social emancipation is fruitless. To him, both are complementary to each other, and, so, democracy and socialism can be preserved at the same time, though the movements of progress may be slow.

The existing social system largely based on inequal behaviour patterns should be reformed before any socialist revolution takes place. According to Ambedkar, *Social reform* falls into two different species. One species of social reform is that does not relate to religious notions of people. It is purely secular in character. The second is that which does relate to the religious notions of the people. For establishing socialism, he feels the necessity of social reforms. He opposes a system which prevents the transformation of a society into new techniques of life. He said, "No one can say that to have the problems of social reform put aside is a desirable state of things. Wherever there are social evils, the health of the body politic requires that they shall be removed before they become the symbols of suffering and injustice. For it is the social and economic evils which everywhere are the parent of revolution or decay".[16]

The economic reform alone cannot create a socialist society in India. Ambedkar gives historical evidence that all revolutions have always been preceded by social and religious revolutions. To him, unless socialism attends to social reforms, it cannot achieve its revolution. He believes in adjustment among the social and economic forces of the times, if a true socialist revolution is to be brought about. His socialist analysis includes an observation of social evils and ceaseless efforts to eradicate them. Socialism is a dynamic concept. It has to take note of the eradication of exploitation, the fostering of self-respect, the opportunity of education and employment for all.

Ambedkar stands against all kinds of *social discrimination.* He advocates for an urgent need of bringing about equality of opportunity to the needy and the weak. All citizens should have equal access to all institutions, conveniences, amenities maintained by or for the public. He condemns discrimination against citizens by government offices or by private employers in factories and commercial concerns on the ground of race, creed and social status. He protects all men from Government coercion and social discrimination. Any kind of *discrimination* is a menace to socialism, because it snatches from the individuals their fundamental rights. He not only revolts against social discrimination, but also against the social boycott, which is a powerful weapon in the hands of some traditional higher castes.

Social discrimination and *social boycott* are the enemies of Ambedkar's concept of socialism, because his socialism lays a stress on the need of equal behaviour and individual liberty and respect. He said, "If socialism is a practical programme and is not merely an ideal, distant and far off, the question for a socialist is not whether he believes in equality. The question for him is whether he minds one class ill-treating and suppressing another class as a matter of system, as a matter of principle and thus allow tyranny and oppression to continue to divide one class from another".[17] To him, a true socialist would not tolerate ill-treatment and oppression, because these are opposed to socialism.

Ambedkar does not leave agrarian problems untouched. He wants that *agriculture* should be a state industry. His scheme of agrarian reforms is democratic collectivism. It does not stand for the total abolition of private property in land, but the public ownership of agricultural production in that land. His scheme of socialism stands only for the cooperative and collective control of the agricultural industry. Through his democratic collectivism, village landlordism along with many other social evils, may be uprooted tooth and nail, by peaceful and legitimate means. The idea of democratic collectivism has won over the majority of the people in all industrial and agricultural organisations. His democratic collectivism, far from destroying man's right to private property, has rather revived it, not in the antiquated individualistic form of letting each man retain his own property, which is difficult in state socialism and its division of labour, but in the giving to every man a claim upon the equivalent of what he has done and produced.

Labour is eminently respected in Ambedkar's social life. Labourers are to be given their due wages besides many other social and economic facilities. They should not feel that they are mere servants of the propertied classes. He said, "Labour may ask the moneyed classes a pertinent question saying: if you do not mind paying taxes to meet the expenditure on war, why do you object to raising funds when their purpose is to raise labour standard? How many uneducated persons could have been educated and how many sick persons could have been restored to health, if the money spent on war had been spent on public welfare".[18]

Ambedkar does not believe in the *annihilation* of moneyed classes, but he wants a radical change in their attitude towards human affairs. They should develop a sense of social responsibility and social philanthropy in the use of their money. He has no liking for a system which regards social inequalities and economic disparities as predestined for certain classes. He does not find in the trusteeship theory any solution to the socialist problems. The moneyed classes suffer from an unlimited sense of property and possession. He said, "The idea of trusteeship—as a panacea and by which the moneyed classes will hold their properties in trust for the poor, is the most ridiculous. . . All that one can say about it is that if anybody else had propounded it the author would have been laughed at as a silly fool, who had not known the hard realities of life and was deceiving the servile classes by telling them that a little dose of moral rearmament to the propertie classes those who by their insatiable cupidity and indomitable arrogance have made and will always make this world a vale of tears for the toiling million—will recondition them to such an extent that they will be able to withstand the temptation to misuse the tremendous power which the class structure gives them over servile classes".[19]

Ambedkar observes that the rural areas in many parts of the country have been dominated both politically and economically by landlords and money-lender. He asks the people to start the reclamation of waste land in rural areas forcibly, if Government does not manage to give them employment. For the welfare of the people living in bigh cities and small towns, industrialisation is essential. Without doing so, there can be no advancement of society. The key objective of his economic programme is an effective working balance between urban and rural development. He holds that a comprehensive programme of land reform is a political and economic must. The most important problems of rural areas are not only the economic advancement and educational facilities, but also vigorous campaign against caste evils, because caste consciousness hampers all economic growth. It creates conditions which are harmful for collective efforts in agriculture and other activities.

Ambedkar does not accept *Marxism* as it is. Though he accepts Marx's interpretation of history partially, yet he differs from him on many points. In his social organisation, man occupies an important place. To him, the impersonal forces are a determining factor cannot be denied. But that the effect of impersonal forces depends on man must also be admitted. It is man who controls some of the impersonal forces and makes possibilities for instruments and machines which are the basis of modern culture and civilisation. Ambedkar lays complete faith in man and his ability to control economic forces in harmony with social problems. He differs from Marxism which regards economic relations as the be-all and end-all of human life. But Ambedkar accepts much of the Marxist philosophy without any difficulty, such as the class-struggle and exploitation theory.

Ambedkar does not agree with the Marxist ideas of the "curtailment of human freedom" and "the violent method of social change." There is no liberty for independent thought and expression in *Marxism*. To

Ambedkar, human freedom is the most essential part of society. Without human liberty, there cannot be a life of mental satisfaction. To him, mere material satisfaction is not sufficient. The way and means, which Marxists wish to adopt in order to bring about communism, are not dear to Ambedkar. He believes in non-violent methods of persuasion, moral teaching and love. He wants to conquer his opponents by inculcating in them the Buddha's doctrine that love can conquer any thing, and not power. He adhered to the principle that the world cannot be reformed except by the reformation of the mind of the man and the mind of the world.

Force, violence and killing of the opposed, as the means of social change, long appeared to Ambedkar, as erroneous and inhuman. He believes in peaceful methods to bring about prosperity to the underdog. He never advocated violence for realising the goal of independence. He never incited his people to do any harm and gain thereby something for themselves. He said, "Do not be allured by the Communist success, I am quite confident that if we all become one tenth as enlightended at the Buddha was, we can bring about the same results by the methods of love, justice and good-will".[20] His theory of state socialism has a peculiar merit in contrast to the theory of scientific socialism of Marx. State socialism can be implemented through legislative methods by the public men without any bloodshed and travail. Whereas scientific socialism is unable to do so by peaceful means.

Ambedkar believes in the intelligence of the modern mind of the man. Morality is God and social service his religion. He takes most of his ideas from the practical idealism of Buddhism. His Social Humanism attaches great importance to social, political and economic relations. His theory of socialism does not ignore human values. All values that we find in his political thought are both extrinsic and intrinsic. His political thought has given due importance to organic values He said, "You should care more for your material good than for spiritual food. You do not get food to eat, clothes to wear, opportunities of educating your children, and medical help for want of money. You should, therefore, be watchful of the political gains and you must develop your strength and struggle for gaining material advancement in life".[21]

Ambedkar related the human values closely with political power and rights. He introduced them in the Constitution of free India. His humanism and socialism recognise the efficacy of political values and regard a human life as worthless when it fails to achieve the values. To him, a proper understanding of human relations is the key to human progress and peace. More intrinsic than both political and social values are moral values to man. They are virtuous living, good conduct and character. These values are the results of devotion to the highest in life. He said, "Character is more important than education. It pains me to see youths growing indifferent to religion. Religion is not an opium, as it is held by some. What good things I have in me or whatever have been the benefits of my education to society, I owe them to the religious feelings in me".[22]

Ambedkar's concept of society and socialism aims at creating more opportunities for the poor classes, ending inequality based on birth, eliminating discriminatory practices in social behaviour patterns, reorganising the political economy for the benefit of all, maintaining full employment and education, providing social security for the weak and the sick and finally rebuilding Indian society on the foundation of cooperation, love and friendship rather than the division of men into rigid social barriers. His political economy has a moral purpose. It studies economic activity from the point of view of its effect on human welfare.

REFERENCES

1. B. R. Ambedkar, *States and Minorities,* Thacker & Co. Ltd. Bombay, 1947, pp. 30-31.
2. *Ibid.*, p. 31.
3. *Ibid.*
4. *Ibid.*, pp. 31-32.
5. *Ibid.*, p. 32.
6. *Ibid.*, p. 33.
7. B. R. Ambedkar, *Annihilation of Caste,* Katra Jaman Sangh, Amritsar, 1944, p. 40.
8. *Ibid.*, p. 49.
9. B.R. Ambedkar, *Mr. Gandhi and the Emancipation of the Untouchables, op. cit.*, p. 53.
10. B. R. Ambedkar, *Annihilation of Caste, op. cit.*, pp. 20-21.
11. *Ibid.*, p. 20.
12. B.R. Ambedkar, *What Congress and Gandhi have Done to the Untouchables,* Thacker & Co. Ltd., Bombay, 1945, p. 294.
13. *Ibid.*
14. *Ibid.*, p. 295.
15. B.R. Ambedkar, *States and Minorities, op. cit.*, p. 34.
16. B.R. Ambedkar, *Pakistan or the Partition of India,* Thacker & Co., Ltd., Bombay, 1946, p. 237.
17. B.R. Ambedkar, *Annihilation of Caste, op. cit.*, pp. 17-18.
18. Dhananjay Keer, *Dr. Ambedkar: Life and Mission, op. cit.*, p. 372.
19. B. R. Ambedkar, *What Congress and Gandhi have done to the Untouchables, op. cit.*, p. 297.
20. *Buddhism & Communism, op. cit.*, Para. 7.
21. Dhananjay Keer, *Dr. Ambedkar: Life and Mission, op. cit.*, pp. 217-18.
22. Speech delivered by Ambedkar to the depressed classes youth conference at Nagpur in January, 1938.

6

AMBEDKAR ON DEMOCRACY

Ambedkar does not merely talk about democracy. He is more a pragmatist than a theoretician. He is a strong believer in practical democracy. He said, "It seems to me that there lies on us a very important duty to see that democracy does not vanish from the earth as a governing principle of human relationship. If we believe in it, we must both true and loyal to it. We must not only be staunch in our faith in democracy, but we must resolve to see that in whatever we do, we do not help the enemies of democracy to uproot the principles *liberty, equality* and *fraternity*".[1] He extends the hands of love and friendship to all democratic countries of the world. He belongs to the realistic school of political scientists. He has a faith in the virtues of democracy such as freedom of thought and expression without which human life is not worth living.

Ambedkar attaches more importance to the service of the needy and the lowly. He emphasises that such a service to humanity should be regarded as love's labour. Without love and devotion, people cannot hold themselves together for any concerted action for the betterment of human society. To him, self-help is the best help. Without self-help nothing can be attained. Through self-help, man can attain self-elevation and regain his self-respect. To quote Mr. Keer, "Ambedkar has played the part of destiny in the liberation of suppressed humanity in India. So India must learn to understand his life, character and mission and know him as he is and not as he is distorted by his enemies or deified by his devotees."[2] He advises the people that they should cherish a noble ideal and follow the right path. He does not want the people to be satisfied merely with organic pleasures.

Ambedkar does not feel pride in quantity. His main aim of life is to create the best. To him, it is not enough that a people be numerically in the majority. They must be always watchful, strong, well-educated and self-respecting to attain and maintain success. He was very hopeful about the future role of the student community. He said, "I am very fond of teaching profession. I am also very fond of students. I have dealt with them. I have lectured them in my life. I am very glad to talk to the students. A great lot of the future of this country must necessarily depend on the students of this country. Students are an intelligent part of the community and they can shape the public opinion in favour of *democracy, nationalism* and *humanism*".[3] Having deep faith in public service and love for the people, he left the service and took to legal practice and politics. He said, "I began my career as a professor of Political Economics in the Government Commerce College, Bombay, in 1919, after my return from England. But I soon felt that the Government service was no good for a man who wishes to do public service. A government servant is bound by rules of a discipline. He is hampered at every stage in his work of public service".[4]

Ambedkar aspired for having a government of the people, for the people and by the people. To him, *democracy* means no slavery, no caste, no coercion. Democracy is a mode of associated living. The roots of Democracy are to be searched in social relationship, in terms of the associated life between the people who form the society. He is a practical democrat. He finds *illiteracy, poverty* and *caste distinctions* as the positive dangers to democracy in Indian society. He said, "If you give education to the lower strata of the Indian society which is interested in blowing up the caste system, the caste system will be blown up. At the moment the indiscriminate help given to education by the Indian Government and American Foundations is going to strengthen the caste system. Giving education to those who want to blow up caste system will improve prospect of Democracy in India and put Democracy in safer hands".[5]

It is very important to educate the poor masses and develop in them a genuine sense of political consciousness and constitutional temper. Democratic society is not merely theoretical. It is related to the actual conditions of the people. A democratic society must assure a life of leisure and culture to each one of its citizens. Practically speaking in a class structure there is, on the one hand, tyranny, vanity, pride, arrogance, greed, selfishness, and on the other, insecurity, poverty, degradation, loss of liberty, self-reliance, independence, dignity and self-respect. To Ambedkar, the aims of democracy is essentially the practical interest of society as a whole, and not of any class, group or community. He regards democracy as the social organisation of the people. Real democracy is opposed to the suppression of minorities.

The democratic principles of life. liberty and pursuit of happiness are considered to be the essentials of human life in Ambedkar's concept of democracy. He attaches more emphasis to human well-being and human rights. So, his view of democracy opposes authoritarianism, dictatorship, fascism and anarchism. To him, the essence of democracy is that as many members of a society as possible should share in the exercise of human rights. There should be equal opportunities for all citizens and harmony among the claims of each person. He puts a weight of emphasis on equality and liberty of human rights. He wants people to cultivate democracy as a state of mind, a style of social life, which may assure them work and security, proper facilities for education and human rights for all. *Democracy* cannot be conceived as a sectarian or racial thing. He said, "Democracy is not merely a form of government. It is primarily a mode of associated living, of conjoint communicated experience. It is essentially an attitude of respect and reverence towards fellowmen".[6]

Voluntarism means freedom to form associations in various fields of life. It has a very important place in Ambedkar's concept of democracy. The state should not control every aspect of human life. He said, "No law should be made abridging the freedom of speech, of the Press, of Association and of Assembly except for consideration of public order and morality".[7] He emphasises on the need of all kinds of freedom so that people may feel and keep themselves in larger liberties. He seeks help of a constitutional system for protecting the real spirit of voluntarism, that is, only a constitutional government can help the people. Voluntarism can exist only in democracy of the people and by the people. It is the soul of freedom and democracy. He attaches great importance to freedom of thought and expression, movement and association, disposal of property and practice of profession.

The concept of democracy in Ambedkar's political thought refers to democracy not simply as a form of government but also as a form of social organisation. He presupposes social relationships to be founded on the principle of Parliamentary system of Democracy. He has a great pride in the cultural tradition of his land. He said, *"Parliamentary democracy* is unknown to us at present. But India, at one time, had parliamentary institutions. India was far most advanced in ancient times. There are innumerable references in our literature to prove that parliamentary system of Government was not unknown to us".[8] Parliamentary democracy produces the best results in the long run. It gives chances to all and changes itself as the human needs dictate. It embodies the principles of change and continuity. To him, only the spirit of the people can help parliamentary democracy to function well.

Ambedkar was strong enough and appealed to all to maintain the parliamentary tradition of Indian *culture*. Parliamentary democracy ennobles the people by putting an emphasis on self-help, initiative an individual responsibility. It promotes a better and higher form of national character. It is considered to be the best form of government. In it, a man feels that he counts in society and is not merely a plaything. He said, "personally speaking, I am very greatly attached to the Parliamentary System of Government. We must understand what it means and we must preserve it in the constitution".[9]

Parliamentary Government means government by discussion and not by fisticuffs. The importance of free discussion and consent is an essential requirement of popular government. To Ambedkar, discussion and consent are the essential means by which controversial points are settled and resettled. He believes that no human being has absolute truth and the best way to arrive at truth is to discuss things as they are. F.W. Coker said, "Democracy is unrealisable without freedom of political discussion. A right to vote gives a man no real part in controlling government unless he is free to form his own opinion about his vote, to hear what others have to say about the issues, and to persuade others to adopt his opinions".[10]

The fundamental aim of parliamentary democracy is to bring about radical changes in a peaceful or non-violent manner. Democracy is a dynamic attitude towards human life. It attaches a great importance to tolerance and peaceful methods. To Ambedkar, democracy is a form and a method of government whereby revolutionary changes in the economic and social life of the people are brought about without bloodshed. Parliamentary democracy involves non-violent methods of action, peaceful ways of discussion and acceptance of decisions with faith and dignity. Parliamentary system of government needs an opposition and free-fair elections. Ambedkar reminds us that the people have nearly forgotten the necessity and importance of a strong opposition for the fair working of parliamentary government. He opposes those who say that opposition is an evil.

According to Ambedkar, free and fair elections are necessary for the transfer of power from one section of the community to the other in a peaceful manner and without any bloodshed. With a faith in peace and democracy, he wishes the people to have such things now and at any time to come. He appeals to educated and enlightened people to adopt the fair means for a change of government. Unless the people realise that the caste system in harmful to democracy, free and fair elections will not be possible.

The first drawback of the parliamentary democracy is that the movements are very slow. Ambedkar said, "In a parliamentary democracy the executive may be help up by the legislature which may refuse to pass the laws which the executive wants and if it is not held up by the legislature it may be held up by the judiciary which may declare the laws as illegal. *Parliamentary democracy* gives no free hand to *dictatorship* and that is why it became a discredited institution in countries like Italy, Spain and Germany, which readily welcomed dictatorships".[11] He is not happy over such alternative to democracy. He is against *dictatorship*. The discontent against parliamentary democracy is due to the realisation that it has failed to assure to the masses the right to liberty, property or the pursuit of happiness. Democracy in India, is unable to provide the basic necessities of life to millions of people. The success of democracy in India depends upon the satisfaction of these mighty millions.

According to Ambedkar, "The idea of freedom of contract became sanctified and was uphold in the name of liberty. *Parliamentary democracy* took no notice of economic inequalities and did not care to examine the result of freedom of contract on the parties to the contract, inspite of the fact that they were unequal in their barganing power. It did not mind if the freedom of contract gave the strong the opportunity to defraud the weak. The result is that parliamentary democracy is standing out as protagonist of liberty, has continuously added to the economic wrongs of the poor, the downtrodden and the disinherited class".[12] *Political democracy* cannot succeed where there is no social and economic democracy. He said, "Social and economic democracy are the tissue and the fibre of a political democracy. The tougher the tissue and the fibre, the greater the strength of the body politic. Democracy is another name for equality. Parliamentary democracy developed a passion for liberty. It never made even a nodding acquaintance with equality. It failed to realise the significance of equality and did not endeavour to strike a balance between liberty and equality, with the result that liberty swallowed equality and has made democracy a name and a force".[13]

Ambedkar warns the harbingers of democracy that if parliamentary democracy fails in this land, the result will be rebellion, anarchy and communism. He said, "I want you to take not of these eventful certainties and if you wish that parliamentary democracy prevail in this country, if you are satisfied that we will be assured of our liberty of thought, speech and action, if we should preserve our independence, if we cherish the inherent right of individual liberty, then it is your duty as students, as intelligent community of our country, to strive your utmost to cherish this parliamentary system of Government in its true spirit and work for it".[14] He is quite aware that parliamentary democracy is not something which can be created in this land by some magical formula. It can be maintained under guarantees of freedom of speech and criticism together with political and economic initiative for the individual.

There are some conditions on which the success of a parliamentary democracy depends. There should be no perpetual authority to rule. Ambedkar wants something more to question the authority of Government.

To him, Democracy requires that not only the Government should be subject to the veto-long term veto of five years—at the hands of the people, but there must be an immediate veto in Parliament, immediately ready there and to challenge the Government. An opposition is a condition precedent for successful working of democracy. The Government must justify every act that it does to those of the people who do not belong to its party. W. Ebenstein said, "The dogmatic, totalitarian viewpoint holds that there is only one Truth, and from that position to the one-party state there is a direct line. The democratic viewpoint holds that different men perceive different aspects of truth, mainly in the light of their lives and experiences, and that there will be at least two sides to any major question".[15] Ambedkar likes the democratic viewpoint, because it gives respect of opposition party.

There should be *equality* in administration, if *parliamentary democracy* is to function well. According to Ambedkar, equality may be a fiction but nonetheless one must accept it as the governing principle of life. All persons should have equal rights. There should be no distinctions of caste, colour and creed. He does not dilate too much on equality before the law. But what he wants is the equality of treatment in administration. The observance of constitutional morality is another condition for the successful working of democracy. *Constitutional morality* means some conventions that the people must observe. Legally, the people are not bound to do so, but they ought to do so under constitutional conventions. He said, "If you read English history you will find many such illustrations where the party leader have had before them many temptations to do wrong to their opponents in office or in opposition by clutching at an issue which gave them temporary power, but which they refused to fall a prey to, because they know that they would damage the constitution and damage democracy".[16] To save democracy and to strengthen its roots, the people must establish some conventions and follow some principles of constitutional morality.

There should be no tyranny of the majority over the minority, if democracy is to function successfully. The minority must always feel safe that although the majority is carrying on the Government, the minority is not being hurt, or the minority is not being hit below the belt. To Ambedkar, there should not be constant agitation, continuous adjournment motions and violent speeches only for the sake of opposition by the minority communities. Such a spirit in democratic set-up is harmful to democracy. He said, "what happens is that these minorities develop a revolutionary spirit something unconstitutional. It is, therefore, necessary that when democracy is working, the majority on which it is based, must not act in a tyrannical manner".[17] He thinks that democracy does require the functioning of moral order in society, if the people wish to make it an act of success.

According to Ambedkar, "Free Government means that in vast aspects of social life, people are left free to carry on without interference of law, or if law has to be made, then the law maker expect that society will have enough morality in it to make the law a success".[18] In fact, the success of law depends on man and his moral activity. The majority of the people is left to be governed not so much by law as by morality. Law plays a small part in human society, only when there is dispute and disorder. He said, "The only person who, I think, has referred to this aspect of democracy is Laski. In one of his books he has very categorically stated that the moral order is always taken for granted in democracy. If there is no moral order, democracy will go to pieces at it is going now probably in our own country".[19]

Democracy requires *Public Conscience.* Ambedkar said, "Public conscience means conscience which becomes agitated at every wrong no matter who is the sufferer and it means that everybody whether he suffers that particular wrong or not, is prepared to join him in order to get him relieved".[20] He finds an utter lack of public conscience in the people of urban areas, even among the so-called modernists in India. He is well aware that there is injustice in every country but the injustice is not equally spread. Public conscience is an essential quality for preserving the parliamentary tradition. His faith in parliamentary democracy adheres to the the principles of continuity and change. The keynote of human society is social progress and human happiness, and the parliamentary tradition is mostly suited to achieve these ends. His view of democracy developed on practical lines.

Political parties are indispensable in *Parliamentary democracy,* for democracy without a party system is unconceivable. To quote B.E. Brown, "Democracy cannot function in the absence of basic civil liberties—particularly those relating to speech and the press—which enable the community to vindicate itself against the state. Furthermore the right to criticise, if it is to be effective, must include the right to organise opposition through political parties. *Representative democracy* is essentially procedural. It is characterised by free expression, free parties and free elections".[21] At least two parties are necessary in democracy for its frutification. He said, "A party is necessary to run Government. But two parties are necessary to keep Government from being a despotism. A democratic government can remain democratic only if it is worked by two parties—a party in power and a Party in Opposition".[22] Again he said, "safety lies in having two parties there must be an opposition to criticise the government. The Government may otherwise easily become *dictatorship"*.[23]

Ambedkar does not believe in the nominal existence of a *party*. It should have a practical programme. To him, a party must do two things: In the first place it must establish contact with the masses. It must go out among the masses with its wares—its principles, policies, ideas and candidates. In the second place it must carry on propaganda among the masses in favour of its wares. He wants a vigorous propaganda of the party programme in society. A political party is formed by men and their ideas. He said, "Men are mortal. So are ideas. It is wrong to hold that an idea will take roots pro-prio-vigore. An idea needs progpagation as much as a plant needs watering. Both will otherwise wither and die".[24] He does not agree with Mazzini that men may be killed, while their ideas cannot be killed.

Men are not interested in principles and policies but they are interested in accomplishing things. What is necessary for a party is to bring about concerted action. In a parliamentary democracy, things can be accomplished not by individual voice but by concerted action. A party which fails to forge concerted actions has no right to call itself a party. He does not believe in the mere formation of principles and policies, showy purposes and empty politics, but he stands for actual propaganda, mass contact and concerted action for the emancipation and enlightenment of all citizens. The secret of freedom is courage, and courage is born in combination of individuals into a party. He lays a great stress on the necessity of the party system in democracy.

Political liberty means political power to capture the machinery of government. To Ambedkar, the people should share political power in a democratic government. Without sharing such power, the fate of a community may not be bright. He said, *"Political power* is the most precious thing in the life of a community especially if its position is constantly being challenged and the community is required to maintain it by meeting challenge, political power is the only means by which it can sustain its position".[25] He does not want the people to use bad means in order to get political power. He condemns false propaganda, mis-representation or the lure of office or gold for a share in the government organisation. Falsehood and unfair means are the very negation of democratic government. Independent organisation is essential for capturing the political power. He said, "If you are to share political power, you must be organised as one solid unit before you could successfully fight for the due rights in the future governments of the country. I must warn you against having too many leaders who believed in paper bodies and paper parties".[26] The downtrodden communities cannot make any progress without sharing political power. Political power is the key to all social progress. The capture of political power does not mean to destroy freedom and disrupt national unity. It stands for nation building.

Ambedkar fought against *caste and injustice*. He struggled hard to create human rights. He wanted to vitalise the conscience of the people and to mobilise the masses in India, for equal human rights. His ultimate aim of life was to create a real social democracy. he said, "A Democratic form of Government presupposes a Democratic form of society. The formal framework of democracy is of no value and would indeed be a mis-fit if there was no social democracy. The politicals never realised that democracy was not only a form of government: It was essentially a form of society".[27] The concept of his social democracy includes human treatment and human rights to all, without which there can be no sure and stable political life anywhere. *Social democracy* unmistakably involves two things. He said, "The first is an attitude of mind, an attitude of respect and equality towards their fellows. The second is a social organisation free from rigid social barriers. Therefore, democracy is incompatible and inconsistent with isolation and exclusiveness resulting in the distinction between the privileged and the unprivileged".[28] Without the social democracy, neither political liberty nor the unity of the nation can be maintained.

According to Ambedkar, *Political democracy* rests on four premises. '(1) The individual is an end in himself, (2) the individual has certain inalienable rights which must be guaranteed to him by the constitution, (3) The individual shall not be required to relinquish any of his constitutional rights as a condition precedent to the receipt of a privilege, (4) The state shall not delegate powers to private persons to govern others".[29] The dignity of the individual, political liberty, social progress and human rights form his basic decent democratic ideals in the political democracy. These democratic ideals depends on ground plan. The ground plan means the social structure of a community to which the political plan is sought to be applied. He said, "Indeed, the social structure has a profound effect on the political structure. It may modify it in its working. It may nullify it or it may even make a mockery of it".[30]

Democracy should be regarded as both a social ideal and a political method. Ambedkar aims at a real social and political harmony. To him, Democracy should be realistic. It should be a state of social cooperation, a state of service and sacrifice based on human experience. Prof. Dewey said, "The foundation of democracy is faith in the capacities of human nature; faith in human intelligence and in the power of pooled and cooperative experience".[31] To Ambedkar, democracy is nothing if not realistic. His idea of democracy is tinged with social realism, human experience and reason, pragmatic and humanistic outlook on life.

The *soul of democracy* is the doctrine of one man, one value. This principle finds intrinsic worth in the individual personality of each man in political and social relations. This stands for the economic well-being of the people, without which democracy has no value. According to Ambedkar, men are unequal by nature in physical and mental endowments, but this should not hamper the way of democracy. What he wants for democracy is that it should become an *economic democracy.* It means that the economic needs of the people are to be satisfied. He does not say that capitalism is economic democracy. To him, the *soul of democracy* consists in the economic welfare of all men living in a particular society, besides its realisation in political relations. In India, the people have not realised that it is equally essential to prescribe the shape and form of the economic structure of society for the benefit of the majority of men. His soul of democracy is not speculative, but it is closely related to the real issues of human affairs without which no adequate concept of democracy can be conceived.

There is a vast difference between the *law of nature* and *human law.* Ambedkar observes that human laws are not ordained by any God. They are not divine institution. They are simply the results of human activities. To him, in most ancient society, people were aimless and wandered without any definite laws, but they realised as a result of human evolution that they should get themselves united for the peace and orders in society. They settled down in different areas and formed tribes. They started their social life with tribal sense of living. *Tribalism* is the most important characteristic of human society. There was insecurity and fear in the minds of all. The individuals surrendered their natural rights and brought into existence rules for the mutual protection. He holds that law has its sources in human needs. Today, there are many kinds of human laws. The most important among them is state law. He said, "State law is incapable of meeting every situation, because the field of human activity is too vast, too shifting and too complicated. Therefore, he insists on the need of moral law. It is only through moral law that the vast affairs of mankind can be managed efficiently. Morality is the essence of human survival. It governs a large part of humanity. It is the most fundamental element in human life and law".[32]

Ambedkar admits that law may require amendments and these *amendments* should be done with the consent of all men/ Laws are made by man for man. He emphasises the point that law must be the same for all and in the interest of all. His conception of human law is wider than that of many others. It covers the whole moral life of the individual and society. Law is not always a force compelling the individual to discharge his duties but a spirit impelling him to act. In his view, impulsion is more important than compulsion. His conception in based on the consent of the people. His ideas of Constitutional law is based on the diginity of mankind.

Ambedkar'a idea of democracy is largely influenced by humanism. *Humanism* stands against inhumanity, barbarity, inequality, exploitation and all kinds of injustice and persistently demands that social wrongs shall not be permanently tolerated. His humanism is closely related to the actual human affairs. It is not theocentric. It is rather anthropocentric. It differs from the metaphysical principle of *medieval humanism.* He revolted against something against which everybody must revolt. His revolt was against *injustice, tyranny* and *cruelty,* which is essentially a mark of humanistic revolt. His humanism attaches primary importance to man and to his faculties, affairs, temporal aspirations and well-being. Intelligent devotion to human values is the essence of his democracy and humanism.

To quote Nehru, "I imagine that he would be remembered most as a symbol of revolt against all the oppressing features of the Hindu society . . . The main thing was he revolted against something against which we all ought to revolt and in fact have revolted in various degrees".[33] Ambedkar not only offered an interpretation of the world and of human society, but also influenced many changes in them. His influence reached out to millions of people. His was a revolutionary call to the servile classes. His concept of democracy and humanism puts an emphasis on self-help, initiative, individual integrity and social responsibility, which can promote a better and higher form of national character than any other policy whatever. In his political thought, both democracy and humanism strengthen love for the country and brotherhood among the different societies, without which no country can survive and no society can establish right relations between man and man.

REFERENCES

1. Address delivered by Ambedkar at the All-India Depressed Classes conference at Nagpur, July 1942.
2. Dhananjay Keer, *Dr. Ambedkar: His Life and Mission,* Popular Prakashan, Bombay, 1962, p. IX.
3. Address delivered by Ambedkar at D.A.V. College, Jullander on 28-10-1951.
4. *Thus Spoke Ambedkar,* (Selected Speeches), Compiled by Bhagwan Das, p. 32.
5. Dhananjay Keer, *Dr. Ambedkar: His Life and Mission, op. cit.,* p. 488.
6. B.R. Ambedkar, *States and Minorities, what are their Rights and How to secure them in the Free Constitution of India,* Thacker & Company Limited, Bombay, 1947, p. 3.
7. *Ibid.,* p.11.
8. *Thus Spoke Ambedkar, op. cit.,* p. 34.
9. *Ibid.,* pp. 33-34.
10. F.W. Coker, *Recent Political Thought,* p. 387.

11. Address delivered by Ambedkar at the All-India Trade Union Workers Study Camp at Delhi on 17-9-1943.
12. *Thus Spoke Ambedkar, op. cit.*, p. 30.
13. *Ibid.*, pp. 30-31.
14. Address delivered by Ambedkar at D.A.V. College, Jullander, on 28-10-1951.
15. W. Ebenstein, *Today's Isms,* pp. 139-140.
16. *Thus Spoke Ambedkar, op. cit.*, p. 46.
17. *Ibid.*, p. 47.
18. *Ibid.*, p. 48.
19. *Ibid.*
20. *Ibid.*, p. 49.
21. B.E. Brown, *New Directions in Comparitive Politics,* p. 77.
22. B.R. Ambedkar, *Ranade, Gandhi and Jinnah,* 1943, p. 77.
23. *Thus Spoke Ambedkar, op. cit.*, p. 58.
24. B.R. Ambedkar, *Ranade, Gandhi and Jinnah, op. cit.*, p. 83.
25. B.R. Ambedkar, *Pakistan or the Partition of India, Thacker and Company Limited, Bombay,* 1946, pp. 337-338.
26. *Thus Spoke Ambedkar, op. cit.*, p. 51.
27. B.R. Ambedkar, *Ranade, Gandhi and Jinnah, op. cit.*, p. 36.
28. *Ibid.*
29. B. R. Ambedkar, *State and Minorities, op. cit.*, p. 32.
30. B. R. Ambedkar, *Thoughts on Linguistic States,* Ram Krishna Printing Press, Bombay, 1955, p. 34.
31. C. C. Maxey, *Political Philosophies,* p. 690.
32. Buddha and the Future of his Religion, 1950.
33. *The Times of India,* 6-12-1956.

7

AMBEDKAR ON STATE

Ambedkar gives more importance to society than to the state. The State has to provide against internal disorder and external aggression. He does not consider state to be an absolute one. He does not agree with Green, Bosanquet, Hobbes, Hegel, etc., regarding the absolute theory of state. He accepts the idea of state as a human organisation. Every social organisation is more or less a composite organisation. There is a great diversity of populations, with varying religions, languages, moral codes and social traditions, forming a congreies of strong and loose associated groups. He wants that a state should be stable and the people should obey the laws. State organisation is based on obedience to authority. He said, "In creating, moulding, expanding and knitting together political communities, what is more important than force is obedience. This willingness to obey and comply with the sanctions of a government depends upon certain psychological attributes of the individual citizens and groups".[1]

Deference and sympathy are the most powerful factors which predispose a people to obey the authority of its government. Ambedkar stands for the stability of state organisation through deference and sympathy. There should be obedience towards government. He said, "Willingness to render obedience to the authority of the government is as essential for the stability of government as the unity of political parties on the fundamentals of the state. It is impossible for any sane person to question the importance of obedience in the maintenance of the state. To believe in *civil disobedience* is to believe in anarchy".[2] He has a strong faith in the state organisation and its utility for the people. He wants that the people should not submit to the acts of coercion of any government. He holds that the state and its *organisation* are a socially functioning body. It is for the good of the individual and society. He conceives the state as an organisation, the aim of which is—

(1) To maintain the right of every subject to life, liberty and

pursuit of happiness and to free speech and free exercise of religion;

(2) To remove social, political and economic inequality by providing better opportunities to the submerged classes; and

(3) To make it possible for every subject to enjoy freedom from want and freedom from fear".[3]

Ambedkar's political thought is essentially in accord with the facts of *society*. He does not consider the state to be an isolated self-sufficient entity. He relates it with voluntary organisation. He does not regard state as an organism like Green, Hegel and Rousseau. He accepts that the state is a human organisation and because it is human organisation, it has to serve the interests of man and society as a servant and not as a master. The inter-relatedness of man, society and state, stands to reason, to him.

There was a social tendency in Indian society to subordinate the *individual* to the claims of the caste and group. The individual had no right to upset the group. Ambedkar said, "In the ancient past . . . life was tribal in thought and action . . . what was done by one individual belonging to the tribe was deemed to be done by the whole tribe. In all ancient societies, the unit was the tribe or the community and not the individual, with the result that the guilt of the individual was the guilt of the community and the guilt of the *community* was the guilt of every individual belonging to it".[4] The individual freedom was curtailed both by the society and the state to most of the people, there was neither individual freedom nor any social and political rights. He did not appreciate this kind of suppression of the individual freedom. He attaches more importance to the eternal struggle of man for freedom. To him, the true freedom of man is not merely political. It is also social, economic, intellectual and spiritual. He endeavours to reach some balance between the central authority of the state and the liberty of the individual.

Ambedkar protects the individual at every level in every moral and lawful activity from being uprooted and from falling under the arbitrary power of the state. He regards the state as a means. To him, the state will continue to exist as long as individuals, groups or societies exist. It plays an important role in establishing good relations between man and man, society and societies. The state is not an end itself, but it is only a means for the furtherance of human ends in the interests of a better future society. He does not agree with the totalitarianism of Marx and Mussolini. He believes in a balance between the organising power of the state and the driving force of the free individuals. He is also opposed to the Machiavellian principle of state-governing the people and keeping them down.

Ambedkar carved out a golden mean between the unitary and federal forms of Government. He gives his own federal view of Government and state. He said, "I feel that it is workable, it is flexible and it is strong enough to hold the country together both in peace-time and in war-time. Indeed, if I may say so, if things go wrong under the new Constitution, the reason, will not be that we had a bad Constitution. What we will have to say is that Man was vile".[5] The federal state of his dream is not a league of small states, nor are these states agencies of the Union Government deriving powers from it. Both the Union and the State government derive their authority from the Constitution. There is a complaint on the ground that there is too much centralisation and the states have been reduced to municipalities. He said, "The basic principle of federalism is that the Legislative and Executive authority is partitioned between the centre and the states not by any law to be made by the centre but by the Constitution itself. This is what the Constitution does. The states are in no way dependent upon the centre for their legislative or executive authority. The state and centre are co-equal in this matter".[6]

Ambedkar's idea of *federal state* attaches more importance to institutional means for the solution of human affairs. It has adopted a middle way between centralisation and decentralisation of power and authority for the reasons that "(1) there is a clear division of government power between the centre and state Governments; (2) Each government is independent of the other in its own field; and (3) The constitution establishes an independent judiciary to settle the disputes between the Union and the states with respect to the divisions of powers".[7] His concept of federalism means that the state is a federation in normalcy but unitary in emergency. To him, the work Indian Union indicates two things, namely, "(1) that the Indian federation is not the result of an agreement by the units and (2) that the competent units have no freedom to secede from it" [8] His view of federalism is not confederation.

Ambedkar is a practical politician regarding the relations between society and government and state. His approach is realistic. It is based on practical politics. To him, the structure and organisation of the state should be based on facts. The State and Government become intelligible concepts only in relation to the actual conditions of society. A state is realistic and practical when it provides the primary needs of the people. A state should protect its citizens against external aggression, maintain law and order against internal disturbance and guarantee to its subjects minimum standards of administration and welfare, which are expected from a modern state. He does not want any state to restrict the movement of its citizens. The state is not an absolute. It has to obey the wishes of the people. To him, no individual should be disqualified to hold any public office or exercise any trade or calling by reason of his religion, caste, creed, sex or social status. A good state is that which guarantees protection against persecution of a community by another community and also against internal disturbance, violence and disorder, in any part of its territory.

Ambedkar regards rights as natural and inherent in the individual. He has a strong faith in the separation of the government's power and of the allocation of functions to various departments. He builds his theory of social and political organisation around his central concept of the individual and his rights. To him, the state exists only to prevent injustice, tyranny and oppression. The state has to serve the people. He wants that no state should violate the fundamental rights of man. He is opposed to all kinds of discrimination on the ground of race, caste and creed. He holds that society can do nothing without some organised power. He stresses the need not only of constitutionalism in its formal basis, but also of *constitutional morality* and some conventions for the practical success of a Constitution. He wishes a good, moral government to protect the rights of the people in all their legitimate functions. He fought for the rights and rebelled against communal absolutism.

All problems of *defence* depend upon the strength of an army. Ambedkar knows well that an army performs an appreciable role in maintaining internal order and defending from external aggression. He said, "One cannot ignore that what is important is not the winning of independence but the having of the sure means of maintaining it. The ultimate guarantee of the independence of a country is a safe army—any army on which you can rely to fight for the country at all times and in any army eventually".[9] The *army* is the ultimate sanction which sustains Government in the exercise of its authority inside the country, when it is challenged by a rebellious element. He wants a special type of army, which is pure in its conduct and character. He wishes to have a non-political army. He is quite confident that a non-political army can defend India's freedom. He said, "The question is whether Indians will be able to defend a free India. To that, I repeat, the only answer is that Indians will be able to defend a free India on one and one condition alone—namely, if the army in India remains non-political".[10]

Ambedkar warned his countrymen not to have a politically tinged army. He said, "I want to warn Indians against the most stupid habit that has grown up in this country of discussing the question of *Swaraj* without reference to the question of the army. Nothing can be more fatal than the failure to realise that a political army is the greatest danger to the liberty of India. It is worse than having no army".[11] If there is a political army, India cannot have a safe and secure Government. He has a deep faith in non-political army, above the political affairs of its own country.

Law is an important factor in maintaining social peace and justice among different groups of people. To Ambedkar, Law is not only a legal function. It also regulates the life of the whole society and nation as well. It keeps within limits all men irrespective of caste, colour and creed. He said, "All citizens are equal before the law and possess equal civic rights. any existing enactment, regulation, order, custom or interpretation of law by which any penalty, disadvantage or disability is imposed upon or any discrimination is made against any citizen".[12] His faith in individual liberty and dignity leads him to the rule of law. He said, "No state shall make or enforce any law or custom which shall abridge the privileges or immunities of citizens; nor shall any state deprive any person of life, liberty and property without due process of law; nor deny to any person within its jurisdiction equal protection of law".[13] He adheres to the principle of law behind the law. He was very much impressed by the American Constitution in which the concept of law behind the law is to be found.

According to Ambedkar, the possibility of revolt is everywhere if the masses are miserable and poor. Law is an obligation which depends upon the social and moral conscience of the people. He said, "As experience proves, rights are protected not by law but by the social and moral conscience of society. If social conscience is such that it is prepared to recognise the rights which law chooses to enact, rights will be safe and secure. But if the fundamental rights are opposed by the community, no law, no parliament, no Judiciary can guarantee them in the real sense of the world".[14] He seeks a harmony between the people and the legal power of the state. *Law* should reflect the actual wishes of the people. Modern political theory has also accepted that the people and the state are inherently related to each other. Men can develop their talents and abilities within the moral purview of the state.

Religion is an effort to improve the social conditions of the people. This is the most important function of a religion in which Ambedkar is very much interested. The state should guarantee to its citizens the liberty of conscience and the free excercise of his religion including the right to profess, to preach, and to convert within limits compatible with public order and morality. He stands for the religious freedom. He knows that the religious freedom is the soul of Indian culture and civilisation. To him, no individual should be compelled to become a member of any religious association or to submit to any religious instruction or perform any act of religion, without the assent of his conscience. He wants his people to sheer clear of all religious fanaticism. Religion is for man. It has to look after the present needs of people. He wants every religious organisation to be free to regulate and administer its affairs within limits of the laws applicable to all. He looks for harmony between the principles of religion and the laws of the land. Both are equally responsible to enhance the cause of humanity at large.

Ambedkar wants that no individual should be compelled to pay taxes, the proceeds of which are specifically appropriated for the use of any religious community of which he is not a member. He does not favour any religious coercion either by some community or by the state. He has a strong faith in the principle of *secularism.* The state shall not recognise any religion as state religion. It means religious tolerance. *Secularism* to him, is a blend of tolerance, liberty and equality and leads towards a synthesis between nationalism and internationalism, though, even in this rational attitude, some people may discover an element of isolationalism. But he does not become a victim of unlimited tolerance. He does not tolerate wrong ideals and practices.

Ambedkar always looked to the Central government to act as a powerful curb on the provincial majority to save the minorities from the misrule of the *majority*. He said, "As an Indian, interested in the growth of Indian nationalism, I must take it plain that I am a strong believer in the unitary form of government and the thought of disturbing it, I must confess, does not please me very much. This unitary government has been the most potent influence in the building up of the Indian nation".[15] He has a strong faith in the people of India. He wants them to be united. He said, "It is all a matter of temper whether you will abide by the fall of your logic, or whether you will refute it, as Dr. Johnson did the paradoxes of Berkeley by trampling under his foot. I am afraid it is not sufficiently realised that in the present temper of the country, no Constitution will be workable which is not acceptable to the *majority* of the people. The time when you were to choose and India was to accept is gone, never to return. Let the consent of the people and not the accident of logic be the touchstone of your new constitution, if you desire that it should be worked".[16]

Ambedkar wanted to have a *Constitution* in accordance with the wishes of the people and a strong centre to cope with eventualities. He stood for a parliamentary system of government. The parliamentary tradition is not new to the people of India. He said, "Today parliamentary system of government is alien to us. If we go to village, we will find that villagers do not understand what is vote, what is party. They find it something strange, something alien. It is, therefore, a great problem as to how to preserve this institution. We will have to educate public, we will have to tell them the benefit of *Parliamentary democracy* and of Parliamentary System of Government".[17] He is keen and enthusiastic to preserve the cultural tradition of his own land.

Ambedkar conceives three features of a *Parliamentary government,* if it is to function impartially for the benefit of posterity. The first is the negation of heredity rule. He said, "No person can claim to be hereditary ruler. Whoever wants to rule must be elected by the people from time to time. He must obtain the approval of the people. Hereditary rule has no sanction in the Parliamentary system of Government".[18] The second is that any law, any measure applicable to the public life of the people, must be based on the advice of the people chosen by the people. He said, "No single individual can presume the authority that he knows everything, that he can make the laws and carry the government. The laws are to be made by the representatives of the people in the parliament. They are the people who can advice the men in whose name the law is proclaimed".[19] The third is at a stated period those who want to advise the head of the state must have the confidence of the people in themselves renewed.

The function of a true government is to protect the interests of the people at large. A *good government* is always desirable for any country, but good government, to Ambedkar, cannot succeed unless there is *self-government.* He combines good government with self-government. This is always a representative government. He said, "Force, it cannot be denied, is the medicine of the body politic and must be administered when the body politic becomes sick. But just because force is the medicine of the body politic, it cannot be allowed to become its daily bread. A body politic must work as a matter of course by springs of action which are natural. This can happen only when the different elements constituting the body politic have the will to work together and to obey the laws and orders passed by a duly constituted authority".[20] To him, the end is human welfare and happiness.

Ambedkar stood for a *self-government* which should be both efficient and good government. There was no preference either for self-government or for good government. He always demanded self-government and good government. Following Prof. Dicey, he says that the actual exercise of authority by a sovereign is bound or controlled by two limitations—external and internal. The external limit to the real power of a sovereign consists in the possibility or certainty that his subjects or a large number of them, will disobey or resist his laws. It means that even the most absolute rulers cannot change every law at his pleasure. Prof. Dicey says, 'There is an internal limit to the exercise of sovereign power itself. Even a despot exercise his powers in accordance with his character, which is itself moulded by the circumstances under which he lives, including under that head the moral feelings of the time and the society to which he belongs".[21] These two limitations determine the nature of good government.

A good government can be judged by its impartiality and justice, clean administration and physical facilities to the people which go to raise the social, economic, political, cutlural and spiritual standard of the masses.

the ability and efficiency of the governing class are not enough for *good government.* Ambedkar said, "What is necessary is to have in the governing class the will to do good or, to use Dicey's language, freedom from internal limitations arising out of selfish class interests. Efficiency combined with selfish class interests instead of producing good government is far more likely to become a mere engine of suppression of the servile classes."[22] He fought not only for self-government, but also for a good government. He had a deep faith in both self-government and good government.

Ambedkar does not object to place power in the representatives of the people to judge the merits of the government. He looks for the cooperation of the people for the success of government. The idea of opposition for the sake of opposition is perilous. The freedom is not a fulfilment. He said, "It is easy to give power, but difficult to give *wisdom.* Let us prove by our conduct that we have not only the power but also the wisdom to carry with us all sections of the country and to make them march on that road which is bound to lead us to unity".[23] With a deep faith in people's government, he urges the people to have a sense of cooperation with one another. Without cooperation, neither freedom nor unity can be maintained. He has a strong faith in the parliamentary system of government and he does not favour a permanent governing class in a democratic country.

In all countries, their exists two classes—the governing class and the servile class between whom there is continuous struggle for power. Ambedkar said, "The existence of a governing class is inconsistent with democracy and self-government and that given the fact that where the governing class retains its power to govern, it is wrong to believe that *democracy* and *self-government* have become realities of life".[24] To him, democracy and self-government become good and real, not when a constitution based on adult suffrage comes into existence, but when the governing class loses it holds to capture the power to govern perpetually. The principle aim of the servile class should be to dislodge the governing class from its position and to prevent it from remaining as governing class for ever. He does not take a very formal and a very superficial view of democracy by making *constitutional morality,* adult suffrage and frequent elections as the be-all and end-all of a democratic government.

According to Ambedkar, *freedom* must be the privilege of all, and not of the governing class only. It is good, safe and realistic when freedom is shared by all. He stands for a true form of democratic government. He advocates complete cooperation between the different groups of people. There should be no distinction on the basis of the tradition that the existence of servile class is ordained by nature. The people, who are chosen as the representatives should keep their fingers on the pulse of the people at all times. This is what he stands for in the parliamentary system of the government.

Ambedkar vehemently opposes the rule of a single party. He said, "It is undeniable that a party is an essential adjunct to popular Government. But it is equally undeniable that the rule of a single party is fatal to popular Government. In fact, it is a negation of Popular Government. The case of Germany and Italy furnish the most cogent evidence on this point".[25] To him, the one party system creates the possibilities of tyranny as well as the possibilities of misdirection of public affairs. This is an inherent attitude of the one party Government. This will be a form of *despotism*. He does not want despotism in any form. He said, "Despotism does not cease to be despotism because it is elective. Nor does despotism become agreeable because the Despots belong to our own kindred. To make it subject to election is no guarantee against despotism. The real guarantee against Despotism is to confront it with the possibility of its dethronement, of its being laid low, of its being superseded by a rival party".[26]

Despotism means the loss of freedom. To Ambedkar, despotism is anti-thetical of freedom whether the despotism is native or foreign. Despotism begets anarchy. Despotism and anarchy prevail when constitutional order does not exist or when a single party becomes the sole judge of constitutional authority. To him, both are repulsive and are opposed to humanitarian society and government.

Democracy is near and dear to Ambedkar's plans and purposes of life. He does not want *monarchy* and condemns *anarchy* and *dictatorship*. In both, liberty is lost. He knows well that these forms of government are incompatible with human dignity and liberty. Social unity among the people consists in the social need for protecting the best, having common rules of morality and safeguarding the growth of the individual. He said, "The *majority rule* is not accepted as a principle but it is tolerated as a rule. I might also state why it is tolerated. It is tolerated for two reasons: (1) because the majority is always a political majority; and (2) because the decision of a political majority accepts and absorbs so much of the point of view of the minority that the minority does not care to rebel against the decision".[27]

Ambedkar is aware of the fact that the majority rule may result in oppression of the individual or minorities. His main concern is to safeguard the individual as against the tyranny of the majority. To him, every constitution must have what the Americans call checks and balances, if democracy is not be overwhelmed by the enemies of democracy. But it must be determined by two considerations. He said, "The first is the necessity of establishing a correlation between the *Political Constitution* and social institutions of the country, if democracy is to be real. As the social institutions of countries differ in their form, the checks and balances in its Political Constitutions must also differ. The second is the necessity of providing a firm flooring to the servile classes against the possibility of their being pressed down by the governing classes, by reason of their superior power".[28] So he protects the minorities from being coerced and exploited by the majority rule.

As a staunch advocate of parliamentary system of government and as a practical political scientists, Ambedkar introduced this system in the Constitution of free India. To quote Prof. Barker, "I am the more moved to quote it because I am proud that the people of India should begin their independent life by subscribing to the principles of a political tradition which we in the west call western, but which is now something more than Western".[29]

Ambedkar was highly impressed by the *American Constitution.* He fully agree with the view that there should be three necessary functions of government: 1. to make laws, 2. to execute them, and 3. to punish those who commit breach of law. He believes that only by dividing the powers of government each department can function with the utmost ease and effectiveness. The necessary departments are known as the Legislative, the Executive and the Judiciary. He did not favour the executive of the British type for India. He warned that if the British type was copied *in toto,* it would result permanently in vesting the Executive in a communal majority. He said, "The majority in India is a communal majority and not a political majority. That being the difference, the presumption that arises in England cannot be regarded as a valid presumption in the conditions of India".[30]

Ambedkar upholds the American form of Executive as a model and adopts it to Indian conditions, specially to the requirements of the minorities. The American form of the Executive forms a democratic and responsible type of government. The following form of Executive can best serve the interests of a good and responsible government. The Executive is intented:

(1) To prevent the majority from forming a Government without giving any opportunity to the minorities to have a say in the matter;
(2) To prevent the majority from having exclusive control over administration and thereby make the tyranny of the minority by the majority possible;
(3) To prevent the inclusion by the Majority party in the Executive representative of the minorities who have no confidence of the

minorities; and

(4) To provide a stable executive necessary for good and efficient administration".[31]

Regarding the functions of *Judiciary,* Ambedkar said, "Rights are real only if they are accompanied by remedies. It is no use giving rights if the aggrieved person has no legal remedy to which he can resort when his rights are invaded. Consequently, when the constitution guarantees rights it also becomes necessary to make provision to prevent the Legislative and the Executive from over-riding them. This function has been usually assigned to the judiciary and the courts have been made the special guardians of the rights guaranteed by the constitution".[32]

Ambedkar stressed the need for an independent *Judiciary* to safeguard the rights of individuals. When he was entrusted the work of forming the new Constitution, he adopted a synthetic attitude. The present Constitution is a mixture of the American and *British Constitutions.* He has established 'a parliamentary system of Government where the heads of the Executive sit in the Legislative and are under constant scrutiny by it. They are thus not separate from each other as in America where an elected President chooses his own cabinet, no member of which is in the country's Legislative. Having a written Constitution, we have given our Judiciary the power it has in America, to declare Acts of the Legislature invalid, even though the Legislature itself might by fresh legislation or even by amending the Constitution, nullify the verdict of the judiciary, and re-enact the laws so declared invalid".[33] He intends to create a judiciary and to give it ample independence so that it can function without fear or favour of the Executive or anybody else.

Ambedkar is opposed to the policy of complete *prohibition* in India for the following reasons:

(1) An enormous amount of revenue is sacrificed for nothing;

(2) People have not ceased to drink. There is enormous amount of illicit manufacture of liquor which is being sold to the public clandestinely;

(3) The money lost by Government is picked up by the illicit manufacture;

(4) Prohibition has demoralised society. Formerly only male members of the family drank because they alone could go to the liquor shop. Now illicit liquor manufacture has become a Home Industry, Liquor being now made at home both men and women drink;

(5) In addition to the loss of revenue on account of prohibition

Government has to undertake increased expenditure on police to enforce prohibition which, however, they never do".[34]

The policy of *prohibition* is economically not sound. All social and economic reforms depend upon the moral conscience of the people. Government has enacted laws against child-marriage, dowry-system, prostitution, smoking in cinema houses, forced labour, discrimination in public places, untouchability, etc., but these things still exist in our society because people do not understand the importance of these laws.

Ambedkar tries every possible means to disseminate *education* among the poor people. *Education* is a sound basis for making headway in human life. He is always conscious of the backwardness of the poor people in the matter of education. The primary function of education is to initiate the child into the life of the larger community. For educating the poor people, he made many efforts. He organised educational institutions and also established colleges. He laid a greater emphasis on practical education and economic development than on the right of the vote. He holds that the greater responsibility for providing educational opportunities should be that of Government. He wants to solve the educational problem through Governmental efforts and agencies.

Ambedkar wanted that both Government and state must be organised on human considerations so that *humanity* may not suffer long. He has a simple faith of a liberal mind and devoted heart to the cause of the poorest of the poor in the world. He believes in the rejuvenation of some social ideals and political values. His actions are characterised by a sincerity of purpose and a sense of responsibility, a concern for human welfare which constitute the essence of his democratic Government and state. He believes in the value and worth of the individual in society, the touchstone of all true functions of the state.

REFERENCES

1. B.R. Ambedkar, *Pakistan or the Partition of India,* Thacker & Co., Ltd., Bombay, 1946, p. 293.
2. *Ibid.,* p. 294.
3. B.R. Ambedkar, *States and Minorities, What are Their Rights and How to Secure Them in the Free Constitution of India,* Thacker & Co., Ltd., Bombay, 1947, p. 3.
4. B.R. Ambedkar, *Who were the Shudras? How they came to the Fourth Varna in the Indo-Aryan Society,* Thacker & Co., Ltd., Bombay, 1946, p. 219.
5. M.V. Pylee, *India's Constitution, op. cit.,* p. xii.
6. *Ibid.,* p. 267.
7. *Ibid.,* p. 269.
8. S.C. Dash, *The Constitution of India, op. cit.,* p. 124.

9. B.R. Ambedkar, *Pakistan or the Partition of India, op. cit.*, p. 360.
10. *Ibid.*, p. 361.
11. *Ibid.*
12. B.R. Ambedkar, *States and Minorities, op. cit.*, p. 9.
13. *Ibid.*
14. B. R. Ambedkar, *The Buddha and His Dhamma,* People's Education Society, Bombay, 1957, pp. 34-35.
15. *Thus Spoke Ambedkar, op. cit.*, p. 12.
16. *Ibid.*, pp. 13-14.
17. *Ibid.*, p. 35.
18. *Ibid.*, pp. 35-36.
19. *Ibid.*, p. 36.
20. B. R. Ambedkar, *Pakistan or the Partition of India, op. cit.*, p. 362.
21. B.R. Ambedkar, *What Congress and Gandhi Have done to the Untouchables,* Thacker & Co., Ltd., Bombay, 1945, p. 240.
22. *Ibid.*
23. *Thus spoke Ambedkar, op. cit.*, p. 100.
24. B.R. Ambedkar, *What Congress and Gandhi have done to the Untouchables, op. cit.*, p. 208.
25. B.R. Ambedkar, *Ranade, Gandhi, Jinnah, op. cit.*, p. 74.
26. *Ibid.*, p. 75.
27. B.R. Ambedkar, *Communal Deadlock and A Way to Solve It, op. cit.*, p. 28.
28. B.R. Ambedkar, *What Congress and Gandhi have done to the Untouchables, op. cit.*, p. 242.
29. *Principles of Social and Political Theory, op. cit.*, p. vi.
30. *B.R. Ambedkar, States and Minorities, op. cit.*, p. 36.
31. *Ibid.*, p. 38.
32. *Ibid.*, p. 28.
33. *The Indian Express,* 17-3-1964.
34. B. R. Ambedkar, *Thoughts on Linguistic States,* Ram Krishna Printing Press, Bombay 1955, p. 33.

8

AMBEDKAR ON JUSTICE AND PEACE

Ambedkar does not agree to a glorification of *war* and *violence*. He believes that war is futile, though at the same time, he observes that the problem of war is essentially a problem of conflict. He accepts that war is the root of all sorrow and suffering in the world. A majority of people hate the acts of war and violence, because these acts hamper human peace and progress. He accepts that war causes a great loss to human life and to material prosperity of the people. He does not dilate much on the problem of war. He believes that the solution of disputes and conflicts should be sought on moral lines of thought and action. He does not agree to agreement and negotiation under threat of acts of war and violence. He stands for a peaceful solution of all problems in human relations.

Ambedkar's attitude towards war and peace is based on practical considerations. He supported a war which meant independence, liberty and equality, a good government and a just society for preserving new values of life. He does not compromise with wrong in the name of peace, though the world is torn up by the wrongs of man himself. To him, *peace* obtained by surrender to forces of violence is no peace. He believes that the humanity is now awakened. It should not tolerate the imposition of wrong ideals and ways of human life.

Ambedkar opposes war tooth and nail but he is not a *quietist.* To him, quietism is not a justification for the doctrine of *non-violence.* It has wider implications in all spheres of human life. He believes that success in any work depends largely upon the means as much upon the justness of the cause. To him, the seeker after truth must possess boundless self-confidence which is generated in its turn from the conviction that the end sought is good and just. He attaches great importance to moral necessity of employing different means. He said, "The man who comes to kill you, or to outrage the modesty of a woman, or sets fire to another's house, or commits theft and is killed while struggling to escape dies by his own sins as all aggressors and wicked men do. If wounding one's feelings is violence, Gandhi's satyagrah is also based on violence. Truly speaking, the law should be non-violence wherever possible, violence whenever necessary".[1]

Ambedkar has a deep rooted faith in the goodness of non-violence. He fully agrees with Sant Tukaram that destruction of the wicked is also a form of non-violence. Without the spirit of courage and justice, *ahimsa* or non-violence is an empty shell. His principle of *ahimsa* is derived from Buddhism, which is based on the middle path. His concept of non-violence is based on a clear distinction of principle and Rule. He does not regard *ahimsa* as a matter of rule. He rather accepts it as a matter of principle. he agrees with Buddha who does not ban killing, if there is a need. He occasionally suggests the use of violence. To him, the necessity of violence arises only in self-defence.

The greatest problem in international relations, particularly before the free nations of the world is the expansion of communism. Ambedkar does not like the process through which peace is being maintained. He said, "We want peace; nobody wants war. The only question is, what the price of this peace is going to be. At what price we are purchasing this peace. . . peace is being maintained by what might be called partitioning and dismembering of countries".[2] To his belief, the communist countries are not faithful towards the principle of peace. They believe in the international expansion of communism. He said, "Here you have a vast country, (i.e., Russia) endlessly occupied in destroying other people, absorbing them within its fold on the theory that it is liberating them. The Russian liberation, so far as I can understand, is liberation followed by servitude, it is not liberation followed by freedom. But the point is this—and it worries me considerably. You are, by this kind of peace, doing nothing but feeding the giant, every time the giant opens his jaws and wants something to eat".[3]

According to Ambedkar, communism and free democracy can live together is not true. He said, "*Communism* is like a forest fire; it goes on burning and consuming anything and everything that comes in its way. It is quite possible that countries which are far distant from the centre of communism may feel safe that the forest fire may be exitinguished before it reaches them or it may be that the fire may never reach them. But what about the countries which are living in the vicinity of this forest fire? Can you expect that human habitation and this forest fire can long live together?"[4] To him, the people must not forget that in the foreign policy of a country, the geographical factor is one of the most important factors. The principle of co-existence seems to be a principle which has been adopted without considering the geographical factors surrounding India's borders.

Ambedkar is opposed to the policy of appeasement and co-existence. He does not see any harm in becoming the member of organisation like SEATO. The SEATO is not an organisation for committing aggression on any other country. The SEATO is an organisation for the purpose of preventing aggression on free countries. The strength of SEATO can help India in preventing the aggression from communist countries. The foreign policy of India largely depends upon the *Panchsheela.*

Ambedkar believes that principles have little value in the international relations. He said, "Principles are undoubtedly very valuable, but I take it politicians have a great dislike for principles, particularly politicians who are dealing with foreign policy. They like to deal with things ad hoc, each transaction by itself, without any underlying principle".[5] He is not a pacifist. He wants to protect his country and make her prepare for war, if she is attacked. She should be prepared for meeting any contingency. He does not oppose peace, if peace is just and honourable. He wants courage, faith and forbearance to arm the human knowledge that guides and leads the people to sincere search for peace and freedom. He does not like *hypocrisy* in the name of peace and liberation.

Ambedkar cannot be regarded as a reactionary. He did never try to recoil progressive steps and did not oppose any scientific outlook shown by any man. He is not a *reactionary.* He is a rebel, and more accurately, he is a revolutionary. He was non-conformist Hindu in his earlier days of life and did not allow anybody to interfere with his own way of reforming things in Hindu society. He was not concerned merely with his own *freedom* and *equality.* He openly stood for the freedom of all. He was a rebel of social type as distinguished from the social one. N.K. Devaraja said, "Criminals such as thieves and murderers belong to the social type. A latently social rebel is one who protests against unjust or undesirable restrictions imposed by society. A person of this type arouses sympathy, and even admiration, in a section of the society, though he may be alone or the first to voice the protest".[6]

Ambedkar protested against the social tyranny and oppression of *Hindu Soceity.* He awakened those who needed help for revolting against inhumanity and barbarity of man by man, of class by class. He takes a broad view of human revolution. To him, human revolution is one of the most needed and fundamental forces of mankind which shape history. Revolution means a better change of life from barbarism to humanism, from violence to peace and mutual adjustment. He was not a man to be frightened at the idea of any revolution. To him, without change, there can be no human progress. He admits that since man has evolved, change is necessary.

Society needs certain standards of living and relationship. The recognition of this principle is most useful for every society. Ambedkar fully believes in the overhauling of old sets of values, if they are really harmful. To him, it is better to bring about a measured and planned revolution in an educated society. He does not like the idea of bloody revolution simply it can give quick results. Change of mind and heart is necessary for permanent effect of revolution on men and women. He is not merely a believer in rebellion and revolution, but also a man of practical habits in life. He does not keep any secret in life.

The ultimate aim of *revolution* and change is to understand man and accordingly mould the institutions. It means the human freedom. Ambedkar stands for the freedom of all men. The aim of revolution is to establish a creative and progressive society for the happiness of all men and women without any unnatural distinction of caste, status and creed. To him, revolutions are inevitable. The ultimate aim of any revolution must be the elimination of vested interests and exploitation and an appropriate distribution of opportunities and facilities that make human life happy. He was not a terrorist. He did not believe in the revolution of Hitler and Mussolini. He condemned the method of terrorism. Neither he was a terrorist nor did he advise his people to adopt such means for bringing about change and revolution. He admired brave and courageous men.

Ambedkar expresses his unflinching faith in the role assumed by norms in integrating a society, nevertheless, he categorically argues for the formation of new norms to fulfil the certainly changing social needs of the society. Exact justice can be maintained only if a society has a harmony between the real and the ideal. It would act against the principle of justice, if a society raises the real, namely, existence of different classes, to the status of an ideal. The principle underlying his notion of justice demands reconciliation and adjustment, change and transformation of wrong ideals and preservation of right norms and principals of social living.

There are two views of the relation between *society* and the *individual*. Thinkers like Fichte and Hegel maintained that society is a sort of entity existing independently of individuals and in a real sense of superior worth. On the other hand, thinkers like Locke maintain that society is nothing more significance than a name for a group of individuals, who alone are of significance and whose interests are alone based in the social order. Neither of these view of society is acceptable to Ambedkar. Society exists in individual social being, and he accepts that the individual by nature is a social animal. As a humanist, he does not believe either in the superiority of social order or in the superiority of individual; society exists in the individual and the individual cannot live without society. He believes in an integrated view of man and society.

Human justice and progress are closely related with man's freedom of thought. To Ambedkar, the conflict between *conservatism* and *radicalism* may be overcome by adopting the golden mean. The golden mean lies in a synthetic outlook on life. According to Ambedkar, the worship of past traditions and beliefs is not good or in the interest of social development, when they have become outmoded and creating forces of disruption and disunity, fear and frustration. He adopts a pragmatic attitude and asks the people to conserve only that which is profitable and workable in a satisfying way. He does not want the total rejection of the past traditions. He wants protection, revision as required, and rejection if necessary, according to the time, expediency and circumstances in human society.

Ambedkar does not stand for the absolute freedom to the individual. He wants certain limitations regarding the exercise of the freedom of thought, though without individual insight and intelligence, there can be no social advancement. To him, conservatism must admit that the revision, even rejection if necessary, must be made in old standards and values in the light of new insights, discoveries and inventions. He offers a synthetic outlook to overcome the evils of extremism.

Ambedkar believes that men are not equal. Some are robust, others are weaklings. Some have more intelligence, others have less. All men differ in many respects. But all they have to enter into what Darwin calls the struggle for existence and survival of the fittest. Only the fittest tend to survive. To Ambedkar, this is because of the rule of inequality. He said, "In the struggle for existence, if inequality be recognised as the rule of the game, the weakest will always go to the wall. Should this rule of inequality be allowed to be the rule of life?"[7] A society, which does not preach equality, between man and man, woman and man, is opposed to the principle of social justice. It is not worth surviving. he has a deep faith in practical discipline and wisdom which the principle of equality between man and man obtains from the demand made upon the people to exercise some moral function.

The principle of equality is the basis of all democratic institutions. It needs protection from all persons who believe in love and justice. Ambedkar said, "The best of men cannot be moral, if the basis of relationship between them and their fellows is fundamentally a wrong relationship. To a slave his master may be a better or worse. But there cannot be a good master. A good man cannot be a master and a master cannot be a good man".[8] Caste and social justice cannot co-exist. He said, "To a low caste man a high caste man can be better or worse as compared to other high caste men. A high caste man cannot be a good man in so far as he must have a low caste man to distinguish him as high caste man. It cannot be good to a low cast man to be conscious that there is a high caste man above him. I have argued in my speech that a society based on *Varna* or caste is a society which is based on a wrong relationship".[9]

In the Hindu social system, social status is ascribed to a man on his birth in a particular high or low caste. Ambedkar said, "One is a Brahmin because he is born of *Brahmin* parents. One is *Kshatriya* because he is born of Kshatriya parents. One is a Vaishya because he is born of *Vaishya* parents. And one is a *Shudra* because he is born of Shudra parents".[10] His doctrine of social relationship differs fundamentally from the traditional theory. His principle of justice puts weight on the achievement of man as a major yardstick. To him, there is no one outcaste by birth and no one is noble by birth. There is no predetermined social status to any one.

Ambedkar did not care for the credit every progressive society must give to its rebels. His aim was to make the people realise that they were living in a sick society which caused decadence and danger to the health and happiness of all people. He opens the corridors of the temples of education and knowledge to all. He asks the people to develop their thinking. He is more concerned with the use of knowledge and education. Education must teach man to know what is wrong and what is right. The society that he conceives is based on perfect justice with love to all and malice toward none.

According to Ambedkar, the theory of *Chaturvarnya* is full of social barriers. It has to satisfy at least three conditions. He said, "(1) It must be composed of four classes and only four. (2) The interelations of these classes must be regulated by the principle of graded inequality. (3) Each class must engage itself in an occupation assinged to it".[11] In such a social organisation individuals are not to be found on equal social footing. This system is rooted in inequality. He opposes its root and branch. In his social engineering, there is no caste, no inequality; no superiority; no inferiority; no suppression; and no exploitation; all persons are equal. To him, the new society should be organised on equality and the absence of caste. He does not undermine the importance of the individual in relating exigencies to new social rules. He believes in the intrinsic worth of each person and right ordering of social relations. He fought against social barriers and founded social justice on the principles of liberty, equality and fraternity.

According to Ambedkar, man is responsible for maintaining justice and peace in human society. No one can escape from the bearings of his actions. Man's actions also affect the social environment. There is a mutual effectuation between man and society. To him, the behaviour patterns of man are responsible for any state of affairs in society. There is no supernatural being, authority or power, which is to function for moral decency in human society. Justice, peace and moral order, all stand for righteousness. Righteousness means right relations between man and man in all spheres of life. To the men, living together, morality is essential. They need it for establishing good relations. He regards morality as the basis of all justice and human relations. Morality arises from the direct necessity for man to love man. It does not require the sanction of God. It is not to please God that man has to be moral. It is for his own good that man has to love man.

According to Ambedkar, a sense of sacredness in morality can help man to obtain right relations in society. *Sacredness* carries a different meaning. In Hindu society, sacredness means something divinely ordained, which cannot be changed in any way, at any time. To him, sacredness stands for something common or universal. It is not a divine or mystic source of human energy. It is a dynamic concept and not a static one. Three factors are responsible for making morality sacred. The first is the social need for protecting the best. The root of this factor lies in Darwin's theory of the struggle of existence and the survival of the fittest. The second factor is the feeling of common good. It plays an important role in making morality universal. The third factor is to safeguard the growth of the individual. Under group morality, the interests of the individual are not safe.

According to Ambedkar, "The group set-up prevent an individual from acquiring consistency of mind which is possible only when society has common ideals, common models. His thoughts are led astray and this creates a mind whose seeing unity is forced and distorted. Secondly, the group set-up leads to discrimination and denial of justice".[12] The primary aim of his moral *universalism* is to establish and maintain justice within an integrated society and a sane state. To him, the best social scheme is that which gives each individual the opportunity and facilities for moral development and cultivation of mind. In this sense, he emphasises the need of the principle of distributive justice which extends to provide suitable accomodation, a suitable supply of water and light, libraries, schools and many other conveniences to all.

Ambedkar does not take any supernatural view of *evil.* He finds evil in human society. His view of evil is more social than metaphysical, more practical than theoretical. According to him, evil is the perverted form of social relations. When right relations between man and man, are twisted for personal gain and group interest, evil comes into being. It denies justice and creates confusion and chaos. Man has a free will. Free will consists of desire and choice. Evil is found in social and moral relations among human beings, like caste and untouchability. *Evil* is not prior to man and society. Evil is possible only where more than one man live together. When there is no man there is no social relation and, therefore, there is no evil. Human relations are the positive source of social evils.

Common rules of *morality* are necessary for establishing right relations among men. Ambedkar's concept of evil is empirical and rational not mystical and idealistic. Selfish desire is the basis of evil. Evil itself does not exist so long as human relations are right. Evil stands as a conflict of individual desires and a perversion of right social relations. In today's society, corruption, nepotism, favouritism and dishonesty are the expression of man's inner frustration and unsatisfaction arising out of distorted view of right relations. Self-contentment and self-control are the virtues which can help man to do justice for others.

The Republican party was founded by Ambedkar. He was also the founder of All-India Scheduled Caste Federation. He formed a purely political organisation the doors of which are open to all irrespective of any distinction based on caste, colour and creed. The guiding policy of this new organisation is governed by the following principles:

(1) It will treat all Indians not only as being equal before the law but as being entitled to equality and will accordingly foster equality where it does not exist and uphold it where it is denied.

(2) It will regard every Indian as an end in himself with a right to his own development in his own way and the state only as means to that end.

(3) It will sustain the right of every Indian to freedom-Religions, Economic and Political-subject to such limitations as may arise out of the need for the protection of the interests of other Indians or the State.

(4) It will uphold the right of every Indian to equality of opportunity subject to the provision that those who have had none in the past shall have priority over those who had.

(5) It will keep the state ever aware of its obligation to make every Indian free from want and free from fear.

(6) It will insist on the maintenance of liberty, equality and fraternity and will strive for redemption from oppression and exploitation of man by man, of class by class and nation by nation".[13]

The Republican Party stands for the parliamentary system of Government as being the best form of Government both in the interest of the public and in the interest of the individual. It is ready to adopt any plan of social and economic betterment of the people irrespective of its origin and provided it is consistent with its principles. The programme of the party includes the removal of poverty, the control of the growth of population, the reconstruction of agriculture, the spread of education, the emancipation of the weaker sections through education, services and economic well-being. To this party, the remedy against poverty is more production and not the pattern of production. For the control of population, it believes in an intensive propaganda in favour of birth control.

The Republican Party stands for National Integration by solving the problem of *linguism, casteism* and *communalism.* It says that casteism is like a cancer, which eats into the vitals of society most unconsciously. Casteism is the denial of social justice. It believes that social justice can secure complete emotional integration of the people of India. Regarding resources, the party suggests re-levy of salt tax, abolition of prohibition and saving of excise revenue, nationalisation of Banks, increase in the direct taxation and avoidance of waste. It also attaches a great importance to labour welfare.

Ambedkar embraced *Buddhism* in the last days of his life. He said, "I prefer Buddhism, because it gives three principles in combination, which no other religion does. Buddhism *prajna, karuna* and *samata.* This is what man wants for a good and happy life. Neither God nor soul can save the society".[14] He wanted to bring peace and justice in the world through the Buddha's religion of humanity. He said, "If the younger generation of the Buddhist countries are not able to appreciate that Buddhism supplies a way of life which is better than what is supplied by the communist way of life, Buddhism is doomed. It cannot last beyond a generation or two. It is, therefore, quite necessary for those, who believe in Buddhism, to tackle the younger generation, and to tell them whether Buddhism can be a substitute for communism. It is then only that Buddhism can hope to survive".[15] Buddhism is a complete substitute to communism. It is unnecessary for the Buddhist people to go to communism.

According to Ambedkar, "Buddhist countries that have gone to communism, do not understand what communism is. Communism of the Russian type aims at bringing it about by a bloody revolution. The Buddhist communism brings it about by a bloodless revolution. The South-East Asians should beware of jumping into the Russian net. All that is necessary for them is to give political form to Buddha's teachings".[16] To him, communism is not a remedy for the removal of poverty. He said, "*Poverty* there is and there will always be. Even in Russia there is poverty. But poverty cannot be an excuse for sacrificing human freedom. Once it is realised that Buddhism is a social gospel, its revival would be everlasting event".[17]

The humanist political thought of Ambedkar accepts good and evil as two distinct and opposing qualities in human society. They are externally related to each other. His humanism would encourage each man to adopt beliefs or to accept things which work best for him in society. His philosophical attitude admits a thorough going relativity of human values. He does not ignore individual human interest. His philosophical attitude is a combination of *naturalism* and *humanism*. He does not deny the truth of nature, but as he believes man is essentially a free human being. If man is not apart from nature, he, too is not a puppet in the hands of nature. He does not draw any line between man and nature. He brings man near to the naturalistic view and seeks in nature the values which are beneficial to man.

Ambedkar has a deep faith in both human reason and experience. In fact, a *combination* of *naturalism* and *humanism, rationalism* and *empiricism, nationalism* and *internationalism* is found in his philosophical analysis of human problems. His philosophy of life encourages man to face the great social and moral defects and troubles from which humanity suffers. His philosophy concentrates its attention upon the analysis of the nature and causes of social and moral evils and upon developing a clear and strong attitude towards better social possibilities, understanding and rectifying specific social ills. His political philosophy in particular is a matter of profound human importance precisely because it is empirically founded and experimentally applied.

Individual freedom and common good are the dearest and most precious things in Ambedkar's political thought. To him, political thought embodies a social dynamism, because man is a political animal and a social being. He has brought modern philosophical thought down to solve the political ills of man. He believes that what is political ideal for most Indians will become a social ideal for all. In his philosophy, liberty and equality have a place. He gives the highest place to fraternity. His political philosophy has a deep faith in fundamental human rights, in the equal rights of man and woman, in the dignity of the individual, in the social and economic justice, in the promotion of social progress and better standards of life with peace and security in all spheres of human life. His philosophy is a synthesis of idealism and realism, empiricism and rationalism, naturalism and humanism, materialism and spiritualism, individualism and socialism, nationalism and internationalism.

REFERENCES

1. Dhananjay Keer, *Dr. Ambedkar: His Life and Mission*, Popular Prakashan, Bombay, 1962, p. 91.
2. *Thus Spoke Ambedkar, op. cit.*, p. 87.
3. *Ibid.*, p. 88.
4. *Ibid.*, pp. 88-89.
5. *Ibid.*, pp. 84.
6. N.K. Devaraja, *The Philosophy of Culture, op.cit.*, p. 125.
7. B.R. Ambedkar, *The Buddha and His Dhamma*, People's Education Society, Bombay, 1957, p. 308.
8. B.R. Ambedkar, *Annihilation of Caste*, Katra Jaman Sangh, Amritsar, 1944, Appendix, pp. 16-17.
9. *Ibid.*, p. 17.
10. B.R. Ambedkar, *The Buddha and His Dhamma, op. cit.*, p. 306.
11. D.R. Jatara, *The Political Philosophy of B.R. Ambedkar*, Phoenix Publishing Agency, Agra, 1965, p. 206.
12. B.R. Ambedkar, *The Buddha and his Dhamma, op. cit.*, p. 325.
13. *Election Manifesto of Republican Party*, 1962, p. 1.
14. Dhananjay Keer, *Dr. Ambedkar: His Life and Mission, op. cit.*, p. 487.
15. B.R. Ambedkar, *Buddhism & Communism* (Article), para. 2.
16. Dhananjay Keer, *Dr. Ambedkar: His Life and Mission, op. cit.*, p. 487.
17. *Ibid.*

BIBLIOGRAPHY

Alexander, H., *India Since Cripps,* Penguin Books, New York, 1944.

Alva, J., *Man and Superman of Hindustan,* Thacker & Co., Ltd., Bombay, 1943.

Ambedkar, B.R., *What Congress and Gandhi have done to the Untouchables,* Thacker & Co. Ltd., Bombay, 1945.

Ambedkar, B. R., *States and Minorities,* Thacker & Co., Limited, Bombay, 1947.

Ambedkar, B.R., *Who were the Sudras? How they came to the Fourth Varna in the Indo-Aryan Society,* Thacker & Co., Ltd., Bombay, 1946.

Ambedkar, B.R., *The Buddha and His Dhamma,* People's Education Society, Bombay, 1957.

Ambedkar, B.R., *Mr. Gandhi and the Emancipation of the Untouchables,* Thacker & Co., Ltd., Bombay, 1946.

Ambedkar, B.R., *Pakistan or the Partition of India,* Thacker & Co., Ltd., Bombay, 1946.

Ambedkar, B.R., *Thoughts on Linguistic States,* Ram Krishna Printing Press, Bombay, 1955.

Ambedkar, B.R., *The Untouchables—Who Are They and Why Have They Became Untouchables?* Amrit Book Co., New Delhi, 1948.

Ambedkar, B.R., *The Rise and Fall of the Hindu Women,* Dr. Ambedkar Publications Society, Hyderabad, 1965.

Ambedkar, B.R. *Thoughts on Pakistan,* Thacker & Co., Ltd., Bombay, 1941.

Ambedkar, B.R., *Annihilation of Caste,* Katra Jaman Sangh, Amritsar, 1944.

Banerjee, A.C., *Indian Constitutional Documents,* Mukherjee & Sons, Calcutta, 1948.

Bharathi, K.S., *Socio-Religious Thoughts of Mahatma Gandhi,* Dattson Publishers, Nagpur, 1989.

Bharathi, K.S., *Foundations of Ambedkar Thought,* Dattson Publishers, Nagpur, 1990.

Bhatt, V.R., *The Harijans of Maharashtra,* Taraporewala, Bombay, 1941.

Chintamani, C.Y., *Indian Politics Since the Mutiny,* George Allen & Unwin Ltd., London, 1940.

Desai, A.R., *Recent Trends in Indian Nationalism,* Popular Book Depot, Bombay, 1960.

Ghorpade, A.K., *Dr. Baba Saheb Ambedkar,* Thokal Prakashan, Poona, 1940.

Ghurye, G.S., *Caste, Class and Occupation,* Popular Book Depot, Bombay, 1961.

Gupta, N.N., *Indian Nationalism,* Hind Kitabs Ltd., Bombay, 1946.

Issacs, H.R., *India's Ex-Untouchables,* Asia Publishing House, Bombay, 1965.

Jatava, D.R., *The Social Philosophy of B.R. Ambedkar,* Phoenix Publishing Agency, Agra, 1965.

Jatava, D.R., *The Political Philosophy of B.R. Ambedkar,* Phoenix Publishing Agency, Agra, 1965.

Keer, D., *Dr. Ambedkar: His Life and Mission,* Popular Prakashan, Bombay, 1962.

Kharimode, C.B., *B.R. Ambedkar,* Vol. I, Bharat Bhushan Printing Press, Bombay, 1959.

Kharimode, C.B. *Dr. Ambedkar,* Vol. II, Bauddha Jana Panchayat Samiti, Bombay, 1962.

Kharimode, C.B., *Dr. Ambedkar,* Vol. III, Pratap Prakashan Bombay, 1964.

Kuber, W.N., *Ambedkar: A Critical Study,* People's Publishing House, New Delhi, 1973.

Lohia, R.M., *The Caste System,* Navhind, Hyderabad, 1964.

Munshi, K.M., *Indian Deadlock,* Kitab Mahal, Allahabad, 1946.

Muzumdar, R.C., *Ancient India,* Motilal Banarasidas, Delhi, 1968.

Patwardhan, S., *Change Among India's Harijans,* Orient Longman Ltd., New Delhi, 1973.

Prasad, N. *The Myth of the Caste-System,* Samjna Prakashan, Patna, 1957.

Pylee, M.V. *India's Constitution,* Asia Publishing House, Bombay, 1963.

Rajagopalachari, C., *Ambedkar Refuted,* Hind Kitabs, Bombay, 1946.

Roberston, A., *The Mahars,* Oxford University Press, Calcutta, 1938.

Sanjana, J.E., *Caste and Outcaste,* Thacker & Co., Ltd., Bombay, 1946.

Santhanam K., *Ambedkar's Attack,* The Hindustan Press, New Delhi, 1946.

Sharma, R.S., *Shudras in Ancient India,* Motilal Banarasidas, Delhi, 1958.

Srinivas, M.N., *Caste in Modern India and Other Essays,* Asia Publishing House, Bombay, 1962.

Tiwari, C., *Shudras in Manu,* Motilal Banarasidass, Delhi, 1963.

INDEX